MADE OVER

HOW TO CREATE A POWERFUL BRAND THAT WILL TRANSFORM YOUR BUSINESS AND SAVE YOUR LIFE

Mike Young

FINN-PHYLLIS
PRESS

ISBN 978-0-9998670-8-2 (pbk)
ISBN 978-0-9998670-8-8 (eBook)

Book Cover Design: Sanja Stojkovic

Made Over/ Mike Young. —1st ed.

www.TheMakeoverMaster.com

Contents

If you've taken all the courses, read all the books, bought all the software, and are still struggling because your business just isn't working, I've been there too.

This book was written for you.

WHERE IT BEGAN

My stomach was in knots. I started profusely sweating, and thought I might actually throw up, right there in the middle of my living room. All because the doorbell rang. Our doorbell never rang.

It was July 2008, and I knew I'd hit rock bottom (or at least what I thought at the time was rock bottom). Looking through the window I could see a burly man standing on my front porch. His tow truck was parked in my driveway, and I knew he was there to repossess our only car.

Just twelve months earlier, I was a millionaire. And yet, on this Thursday evening around 5:30pm (when he could perfectly intercept me coming home from work—if I'd had a job to come home from, which I didn't), I was deathly afraid to open my door and be faced with the consequences of my newfound financial reality. I was dead broke. I remember thinking two things as I grabbed the door handle with my sweaty palms: *How the fuck did I get here?* and *What the hell am I going to do now?*

* * *

Hang on a second; I need to back up a bit. Before I tell you what happened after I opened the door and share the rest of my story, I'd like to tell you how I got there so you have some context and the rest of the book will make much more sense.

My journey toward my ideal lifestyle began years before I realized what I was even setting out to create.

Growing up, I had a one-track mind, and from the age of four to 23, I thought of one and only one thing: becoming a professional baseball player. As a child, I even slept in my baseball hat. During my teen years, I gave up all other sports and approached baseball with a laser focus. I was all in; there was no Plan B. I was going to be a left-handed, Major League Baseball pitcher. In 1993 I attended Portland State University on a full-ride, Division One scholarship. I was on my way.

I was also young and naïve. Like many college freshman, I thought I knew it all and was invincible. I had dominated the sport growing up, and in high school I was 47-3 as a pitcher with a .73 earned run average. I was statistically one of the best pitchers of that decade in Oregon. But everything changed during the last game of my freshman year against our cross-town rival, the University of Portland Pilots. On my last pitch of the season, I experienced excruciating pain, which turned out to be a micro-tear in an elbow ligament. It slowed me down tremendously, and suddenly my college record was a less-than-stellar five wins and twelve losses. It was the first time I considered the idea that my dream of going pro might not come true. My whole identity was wrapped up in baseball. With that micro-tear, I saw all of my dreams, visions of everything I thought I could become, being torn away from me. It was a devastating realization.

After four years, you are no longer eligible to play collegiate sports, so I had to enter my fifth year of college while simultaneously being forced to put my baseball dreams behind me. I had been pursuing a degree in economics (because you have to major in something), but I had never attached any real meaning to a degree. For me, college was the path to a career in baseball. So when my dream ended, college followed suit. I only needed to complete two more terms to receive my degree, but at that point I no longer cared. My baseball dreams were officially dead. I just wanted to get out into the real world and start making money.

THE BEGINNING OF THE AMERICAN DREAM (AKA MY NIGHTMARE)

I had a friend who was making a good living in the mortgage industry, and she told me I would be great at it. Without thinking much about it, I dove right in, and in 1998 accepted a position as a loan officer. I had little-to-no idea what I was doing, but having pursued economics, the area of money was one I understood and had an interest in—as in, I had an interest in making it. As my friend had anticipated, the job was right up my alley. The position was 100% commission-based, but that didn't rattle me one bit. I think I got that from my dad, Wayne. He was extremely entrepreneurial, and I learned how to create and grow a business from watching him. He initially started his own steel company, Brookway, doing rehab on the I-Beams of the Brooklyn Bridge. Then, when I was in high school, he created another business out of thin air, all because of my worn-out baseball shoes.

As a pitcher, I frequently wore through the toe of my shoe by dragging my foot as I threw the ball. We had to ship off my cleats to California to get a piece of plastic put over the toe so that I didn't have to constantly buy new shoes. He saw an opportunity that led him to create a product that was better than what was available at the time. The business, Hurler Athletic Company, is one he still runs, and it continues to grow. He's known in the industry as "The Pitching Toe Guy," and any MLB pitcher who wears Adidas and the majority who wear Nike are wearing his pitching toes. He also services college teams all across America for baseball and softball.

I watched my dad expand his business as he persisted in finding ways to improve his products and services. I think this is why when I started working for the mortgage company, I immediately began to absorb everything I could about the industry. Like my dad, I was constantly striving to do better and improve wherever I could. While I only made $37,000 my first year, I quickly rose in the ranks, and in 1999 my earnings increased to $112,000. By 2001, I was making over $300,000 and maintained that income level for a few years.

Not bad for a college dropout.

I've never enjoyed being told what to do, and growing up, I was always a bit of a rule breaker. Whatever my parents said not to do, I did. When I was younger, they discovered that they could get me to eat my vegetables by saying, "Don't eat that." They learned to use reverse psychology tactics to achieve a desired behavior without having me putting up a fight.

But being in the real world requires listening to your bosses and following a *lot* of rules. So far, my employment in the mortgage industry didn't force me to adhere to too many unbearable guidelines. Besides, by then I was making enough money not to care much. But around 2003, the government put new industry regulations in effect that resulted in a whole new set of rules, more restrictions, and quadruple the required paperwork. Working on a completely commission-based salary was quite entrepreneurial in and of itself. I felt like I was running my own business, much like a realtor does. So when the higher-ups at the company started telling me what to do with regards to my clients' loans and exactly how things needed to be done, I was having none of it.

Not long after the new rules started flooding in, I had a meeting with five co-workers and suggested that we create our own company. We were all successful loan officers, and we were all irritated with the new regulations and limitations. They were on board, and we immediately started working on our own venture. We would follow the industry regulations but cut through the bureaucracy and red tape that we couldn't stand. During that first meeting, we decided to name our new company after a street that one of us lived on. That's how easily Alpine Mortgage Consultants was born.

I've always been willing to just make a leap without worrying too much about what challenges I'd encounter on the way down, not to mention how far down solid ground was.

But I was about to find out.

THE BEGINNING OF THE DOWNWARD SPIRAL

Between 2003 and 2008, we grew Alpine Mortgage from six guys and six assistants to ten offices and 250+ employees. We initially generated loads of revenue, and we were all ecstatic with our newfound freedom as well as our early success. But we hit some sort of a plateau in 2005. I swiftly went from making $350,000 a year to $100,000 to $60,000 to zero. The business had become a cumbersome beast. In the early part of the plateau—when we were still generating loan revenue—I continued to be able to pay myself, but we got to the point where we had to invest all of our revenue back into the company in order to keep it going. We had to cover employees' salaries, licenses, lawyers, overhead, etc. The fact was, we hadn't figured out how to manage the business. The owners who were producing were also dumping all their earnings back into the company. We really screwed up, and I went through a year where I was paying myself about $6,000 per month, but my monthly personal expenses were running nearly $14,000. It was a year of going backward.

Beginning in 2003, I also did three things that, combined, resulted in the perfect storm of deterioration. First, I custom built an $800,000 house, into which I invested about $160,000 cash for upgrades. I then bought two cars worth a combined $150,000. Finally, I married Katie (which was, for the record, one of the smartest things I've ever done, but we paid for most of the wedding ourselves, and it wasn't cheap). The American Dream had snowballed into a financial nightmare. By 2009, on the surface I had it all: a wife, two kids (one boy, one girl), fancy cars, a big house, and my own business. But life had spiraled out of control; my expenses had gone from $2,500 per month (when I was making $30,000 per month) to $14,000 per month (after my income had dropped to $6,000 per month). By 2008, I'd run out of money. I was miserable. I knew I was broke. I'd made well over a million dollars over the previous five years, and in my mind, I'd pissed away or flat-out lost it all. This was the beginning of both a massive depression and a transformative self-discovery period for me.

DEVELOPING A THIRST FOR KNOWLEDGE

Years earlier, in 2004, I attended a mortgage event called Sales Mastery run by Todd Duncan. Being the phenomenal speaker that he is, he had a huge impact on me. He talked about what it takes to be an Olympian, and then spoke about his reading habits and the benefits of continued knowledge and growth. For whatever reason, his message firmly resonated with me.

I was so affected by Duncan's commitment to and belief in reading, in fact, that I went on to read over 1,000 books in the years that followed that event. I'd never been a solid reader. I've actually found ways *not* to read books all my life, and that included cheating and taking shortcuts in school. I'd strategically sit behind the right person during a math test, or I would find ways to read a book's CliffsNotes in order to write the assigned report without reading the entire book. But this was real life, not a test, and I got to the point that I was determined to learn my way out of the mess I had worked my way into.

Despite my dwindling bank account, I came up with the funds necessary to pay other successful mortgage companies thousands of dollars just to sit in their office for a weekend and observe their processes. All I wanted to do was make the business work. I also attended a team training put on by Doug Andrews, author of *Missed Fortune*. They literally handed attendees a manual and said, "Here are all of our operations. Here are our daily habits. Here is our schedule. Here is everything." I went to dozens of such mortgage events (spending money one successfully could argue I didn't have to) to learn from people who had their shit together.

To take the previously detested yet now celebrated activity of reading a step further, we created a book club at our mortgage company so that everybody would be in a constant state of learning. We wanted to become a mortgage company that was different from the others, to grow beyond the standard of processing loans. We started studying and focusing on financial literacy and education. I went through a year wherein I read every single book written by Dave Ramsey, Suze Orman, Rick Edelman, and other standouts in the financial industry. I solicited everyone's opinion on how money worked so I could form my *own* opinion about how money worked.

Surprisingly, I really dug into learning. I developed a habit around continuing to improve by attending conferences and masterminds as often as I could. From 2006-2008, I was consuming knowledge with the specific intent to fix the growing problem we had at the mortgage company. I knew the business was going south, and fast, so I went to a mortgage conference in Las Vegas that was run by Stephen Marshall. I had taken a course by Stephen and a guy named Jim McQuaig that focused on college planning strategies. It essentially detailed how to use mortgages in tandem with overall financial planning—how to marry the two concepts. There were a couple thousand people at the conference, and Tony Robbins was one of the speakers. During one of the breaks, I met Todd Ballenger, who would become my first true mentor. He had a small booth at the event and was one of the event's sponsors; his company was named Kendall Todd. He had written a book titled *Borrow Smart Retire Rich*, and the only product he was pitching was his mentorship program. He was trying to find forty people who were willing to pay him $12,000 to go through his year-long mastermind. I talked with him at the event and told him how much I was struggling—he was such a great guy, really down-to-Earth—and he said, "I think I can help you." So I enrolled in his program. The conference cost about $1,000 to attend, plus travel, and I was there with the sole intent of figuring out how to fix my business. Todd reinforced that his program would enable me to be surrounded by forty other mortgage company owners with whom I'd be able to work with to figure it out.

Within the course of the mentorship program, Todd truly wanted us to understand some fundamental lessons he'd learned around acquiring and living your ideal lifestyle—a principle he referred to as VERITAS (Harvard University's Motto). He talked about the concept of an ideal lifestyle as well as the cost that comes with faking that lifestyle by commuting for hours, putting on a suit and tie every day when it wasn't necessary. The concept completely blew my mind. It was the first time I'd heard someone as successful as he was propose that a lifestyle completely in line with my rule-breaker approach was truly possible.

Another program intrigued me at that same time—Dan Sullivan's Strategic Coach program—and it beautifully complemented Todd's mentorship program. Strategic Coach was focused on concepts related to how to be a better entrepreneur as opposed to how to be a better mortgage business owner. The mentorship program was heavily focused on Todd's message of getting us to our ideal lifestyle and thinking about time and money differently, while Strategic Coach was about becoming a more efficient entrepreneur. It detailed systems and concepts. The requirement to become a coach within this program is going through three years of the program and proving Dan Sullivan's concepts in one's own business practice. Todd Ballenger had done this and was offered the opportunity to become a certified Strategic Coach, but he turned it down. He just decided it wasn't for him.

I found Todd's overall journey fascinating. At one point, he received an offer to purchase his mortgage company, and his options were to accept $25 million in stock options or $5 million in cash. He took the stock options. He said to us, "I'm telling you, $25 million is not the answer. A lot of you are going for $25 million, and I'm telling you, I've been there, and it doesn't change anything. You can't buy and eat five hundred Whoppers." He went from not having $25 million to having it in an instant, but nothing about his life fundamentally changed. It was at that point in the telling of his story that my concept of and thoughts around money abruptly changed. Todd introduced me to study from some equally deep thinkers, including Joe Dominguez, each of whom had poignant worldview thoughts around how both money and people work.

There was a period of time during the mentorship program when we were studying and talking about what I can only describe as minimalism. There was a course that one of the guys, Tom Griffith (who would become my business partner from 2010-2015) created called "What Is Enough?" The focus was money. We were asked a number of questions such as, "How much money do you need to retire?" Everyone was throwing out random numbers: "I need $5 million" or "I need $10 million." Todd introduced the concept of questioning whether or not those assumptions were true. He talked about the fact that one could take an honest look at their lifestyle and recognize that they only needed $500,000. Joe Dominguez, who wrote *Your Money or Your Life* (which I want to read every year for the rest of my life) figured out how to live on a fixed income of $27,000 per year, and then strategized his investments in such a way that they kicked off $27,000 per year of guaranteed interest. He retired at 33 years of age.

A speaker named Robert Middleton, whose area of expertise was marketing, frequently asked, "Is what you assume to be true actually true?" It challenged a lot of my beliefs, and we were encouraged to look at our finances and assess what it was truly costing us to live, down to the professional attire we were buying that we wouldn't need to buy if we worked in a home office. My dollar figure in that box was huge. I easily had $20,000 worth of suits in my closet, and I thought, "Shit, if I worked at home, I wouldn't need any of those!"

We read *Affluenza: How Overconsumption is Killing Us—and How to Fight Back* by John De Graaf, which prompted discussions about tiny houses and what's truly enough. The book really got me thinking about human consumption and the fact that the average American spends more on trash bags than some countries' complete GDP. I thought, "Fuck, we waste a lot of money, and we consume a lot of stuff!" There's a website, thestoryofstuff.org, that compelled me to think about what we're consuming and why. What is enough in terms of money, and how does one save enough that he doesn't have to stress about getting more of it?

When we recognized that we didn't have our ideal lifestyles—even though we were working six or seven days a week, all day every day—we recognized that money was just the vehicle through which we could access the freedom we were seeking. For me, that freedom came down to one primary thing: freedom of choice. I craved the ability to choose when I worked, where I worked, and with whom I worked. I wanted to play by my own rules and had the sudden recognition that I was still playing by somebody else's. This created conflict in my life because it was a painful realization. I wasn't being true to myself. I constantly told people that I was someone who played by his own rules, and yet I wasn't living by example.

I think that, if you'd asked me back then, I'd have said I was passionate about mortgage and financial literacy. Looking back, what I was actually passionate about was creating what I deemed to be my ideal lifestyle. And while, at that time, all outward appearances communicated otherwise, that ideal lifestyle wasn't all about houses and cars. It was about money for sure—but not for the sake of simply having a lot of it. I wanted freedom, and money was the means through which I could have and sustain that freedom. Todd helped me to understand that mortgage and financial literacy represented, at that point in time, the vehicle that could get me where I really wanted to go.

* * *

Here's the deal: If you feel like you've taken all the courses, read all the books, bought all the software, and are still struggling because your business isn't working, I completely get it. I've invested years of my life and over $200,000 of my own money searching for answers. If I shared my thoughts on every course I've taken and every event I've attended in this book, we would be here for months.

When you spend years banging your head against the wall without mentors, coaches, or direction, and you spend 340 out of 365 days of the year in the office working until midnight, you get extremely tired. I woke up in late 2017 and felt confused, isolated, powerless, and alone. I was working harder than I've ever worked in my life, and the results were less-than-stellar.

The journey does not have to take you as long as it took me. It requires time, effort, commitment, and patience, but it is my hope that this book will save you from some of the mistakes I made, and let you in on some of the proactive measures you can take right now to ensure that you get to your goal far more quickly than I did.

My goal is to help people just like you—who deeply want to run their dream business and achieve their ideal lifestyle—shortcut what took me eight and a half years to figure out. My hope is that my lessons learned can help you avoid years of unnecessary struggle. It took me close to a decade to run into the right group of mentors and coaches and be ready to do the work necessary to put all the pieces together.

I wrote this book for you if you are an entrepreneur or business owner who's ready to finally get the business and life you want and believe you deserve. This is for you if you're willing to adjust your mindset and solve any lingering self-confidence issues. If you've had enough of doing it the way you've been doing it. If you have a product or service you feel good about selling, you're ready to prove your business model in the marketplace, and you believe that the money you receive in exchange for your product or service is of equal or greater value than what you're delivering to your clients and customers. If you consistently have clients who want to refer you and who give you rave reviews. If you know who you are and what you represent to the marketplace, and you're ready to tell a lot more people about it. If it all feels so close, but you haven't figured out how to tie everything together to achieve the success you've been striving for. If you haven't started telling a whole lot more people about your product or service because you aren't exactly sure what to do next. If you know you are on the verge of a breakthrough but can't figure out why it's just not working.

If *any* of that sounds familiar, I wrote this book for you.

The guidance within this book will not work for someone who isn't truly committed. The concepts that create The Makeover Method™ are simple, but they aren't easy. If you enter into this process without being truly committed, you won't make progress. If you're not ready to deal with the real shit, admit the truth to yourself, get past your initial mindset blocks, and stop telling yourself false stories, the process may appear to work for a short term, but you won't be happy. You're won't acquire your ideal lifestyle; it will feel as though something is always missing, and at some point, it will implode on you. What it really comes down to is self-worth—to loving yourself enough to allow it to happen and believing that you're worth it.

I earned the title The Makeover Master not as a reflection of the notion that I'm better than everyone else in my area of expertise but because, in addition to making over the business image of my clients, I've been making over every aspect of my own life for years. I had to make over my mindset, my habits, my routines, and my business model. I had to get into alignment with what I declared to be creating.

In the end, it's what saved my life. And, if you're ready, I'll show you how The Makeover Method™ can get you more money, influence, power, and respect with your business as well.

Here's to finally putting it all together and getting the business and life you deserve.

MAKING A DECISION

*You only live once. Decide on the life you
want to create and go get it.*

It was March 2008, and I had been climbing an uphill
battle for three years as far as my company was
concerned. I was absorbing all of the knowledge I
could and spending all of my time trying to find the
solution that would save it, not to mention dumping all of
my money into it. We could see the writing on the wall.
Katie and I sold our custom-built house and majorly
downsized to a townhome in a less expensive suburb of
Portland. We had also become parents—our son, Jeff, was
born a year earlier in March of 2007.

I realized that, when it came to my career, I truly wasn't
living the life I wanted to live. I'd gotten so clear on my
ideal lifestyle, and I'd begun learning from Dan Sullivan,
Tim Ferriss and a few others that eighteen-hour days full
of stress weren't as necessary as I might have previously
thought. I started to again consider the details of my own
ideal lifestyle as well as the most efficient way for me to
spend my time each day. I began to test different ways to
manage my time, and quickly became irritated by how long

it had taken me to learn about and adopt this new mindset. I went down to a four-day work week and actually got more done and felt more balanced than I had when I was working six or seven long days a week! I was efficient enough during those four days that I could turn off my email and phone for the entire weekend. I was documenting all of my time working as well as my output, and I had undeniably proven that I was more efficient with this new approach.

Regardless of my productivity level, I began hearing the water cooler talk from employees as well as my business partners, who were saying things like, "Mike's never here on Friday." Even though I had proven that I was more efficient and getting more done, and they were still talking shit because I was doing it in an unorthodox way! The bureaucracy and structure of all of it had become too much. After all, I created the company so that I didn't have to follow anybody else's rules, and everyone else was still creating rules for me to follow. Just like the mortgage company I'd previously worked for, Alpine Mortgage had grown to the point where it started applying more and more rules and restrictions on employees. Here I was, a partner in the company, and they were still trying to make me follow their rules. My response was, of course, "Screw you. Don't tell me what to do."

It was time for me to make a decision.

I'd had enough. I was miserable, and I was getting closer and closer to quitting even though I was an owner, although I hadn't talked to anybody about that feeling just yet. I came home early from work one day, which, even given my new "work smarter not harder" approach, was unexpected. My son Jeff had just turned one year old, and I remember the day so well because it had such an impact on me.

I walked up the stairs into the main living area, and Jeff was sitting on the floor next to the kitchen table banging on his tiny xylophone. He turned around, looked up, and was so excited to see my face that he put both of his fists in the air and just kind of contracted every muscle in his entire body in excitement while shouting "Eeeeee!" He didn't know how to control his emotions, and this was how they escaped. He ran to me, and I picked him up and gave him a giant hug. That was the moment when I decided, "I'm not going to spend seventeen more years in an office and miss all this time with my boy." I was vividly aware of how much I loved my son and my wife, and I wondered why in hell I was leaving them every single day for huge chunks of time—especially to do something that was sucking the life out of me.

I said, "You know, Kate, I don't think I want to live my life this way, in an office. I don't like the rules they're placing on me. I think I could do something else on my own." Voicing my thoughts to my wife about quitting was the beginning of taking true ownership of the words and concepts that were coming out of my mouth with regard to truly creating a life where I had the freedom to do things my way. After all, if you're running around declaring something, you damn well better be living your life by it. We had already given up most material possessions at this point, but the agony of the way I was spending my days was worse than the pain of monitoring our steadily dwindling bank account.

Katie said, "Just quit. If you don't love what you're doing, just quit. You're smart; you'll figure something out." Plain and simple, Katie was born to be an entrepreneur's wife. Her dad left when she was seven, both of her parents drank too much, and she didn't grow up in the most functional household. There was never a lot of money or stability. She grew up with three brothers—one older and two younger—so she had to learn to fend for herself from an early age. That seemed to ingrain something into her DNA in such a way that the instability of being married to an entrepreneur didn't scare her away. She craves stability because she didn't have it as a child, but it was the stability of a family she desired, not the materialistic lifestyle we are all taught to worship. We decided even before our son was born that she would quit her job and focus solely on raising Jeff because she knew she wouldn't be able to stand being away from him all day. To her, the income wasn't worth the time that she would have to give up being with him. Understanding how I felt because she had felt that way herself, she was able to say, "My whole life has been up and down, insecure, not knowing what's going to happen, so how is this any different? We will be okay as long as we have each other."

Katie is quick-witted, hilarious, and perfectly comfortable being her silly, playful self, but when she needs to stand on her own two feet, can she ever. One minute she seems like the cute, bubbly girl next door, but then she'll say something that makes it immediately clear that she's extremely smart. In our time together, she wasn't ever worried about where the money was going to come from. It's never been about the paycheck in her eyes. It's about time and being present. I quit the next day and was bought out of my mortgage company partnership two weeks later for a single dollar.

DISCOVERING MYSELF

Your ability to articulate what you want in life and why you want it is everything.

The first few months after I quit was an amazing period in my life and one I'm grateful for…now.

It was a hard time because I was on my own to figure it all out. But, the period of time after I quit was the one wherein I really got to know myself and connect with my wife. We talked about and documented our values together. Her view was, if I made $50,000 a year but was there for her and the kids (because, by the way, she was newly pregnant with our daughter), that was far more important than making $500,000 a year and me never being there. So, the focus became, "How can I put those two together?" That's what my "having it all" became all about. How do I have the business while maintaining my health, balancing time with my family, and staying mentally grounded?

I didn't know the answers yet, but I was determined to figure it out and have the answer be one that was on my own terms.

I'm pretty sure all of my old employees and most of my friends thought I had lost my damn mind. From the outside, I was one of the owners of a very successful business. I imagine that people wondered why I would give up ownership in a successful company that so many people liked working for.

I'm sure the common perception was that I had plenty of money and was just bored, ready to take on something new. I can't say for sure though because I never gave anyone a chance to ask questions. I didn't even formally announce my resignation; I just cleared out my office after meeting with my partners and closed the door on that chapter of my life.

The next thing I knew, I was in my home office with no plan or vision of what I wanted to do next. I literally quit with no money, no plan, and no vision. I just knew that my career had gotten painful enough that I would rather have no plan than have *that* as a plan.

My new reality was the exact opposite of my prior existence. It took nearly three weeks for me to decompress from my previous environment. Much like a doctor with a pager, I was used to constantly being summoned, pulled into meetings, and receiving more than two hundred emails on a daily basis. In just one day's time, I found myself sitting in my home office with zero emails, zero phone calls, and zero meetings.

It was a surreal. I'd followed the timeline that society lays out for you: go to high school, go to college, get a job, make lots of money, buy a big house, buy two cars, get married, procreate. And then one day, I woke up and all I wanted to do was stick a sharp spoon in my throat. I didn't just want it all to end, I wanted it to end painfully! That was the greatest mind-fuck of all. I had lived the dream—and I was fucking miserable doing so.

After I quit, I was fascinated by the fact that, out of all my "friends," almost no one reached out. Very few people (as in, less than five) asked me why I quit or how I was doing. Very few seemed to give a shit, and that blew my mind. While it was definitely a hit to my self-esteem, over time I began to realize that most people are so wrapped up in their own lives that they aren't giving much thought to what you are doing with yours. Or, at the very least, not as much as you might think. For three weeks or so I was scared to death, wondering what I was going to do, not to mention what I'd just done. At the same time, I was excited, and I quickly chose to become clear on my true relationships and friends.

Surprisingly, I'd genuinely believed I played a pivotal role at Alpine Mortgage, and that if I left, the entire business would quickly fall apart. That didn't happen, and that reality forced me to recognize that people leave companies—whether temporarily or permanently—every single day, and those companies keep going. That awareness caused my self-worth (my ego) to take its first big nosedive. I genuinely thought I was a critically important cog in the wheel, and I thought I had fifty to seventy-five really good friends. And yet, nobody seemed to care that I'd left, and the company kept going. I got to see what it felt like to witness my death from an outside perspective—like Mike Young the Mortgage Guy was dead—and I was viewing the aftermath, only to see that nobody really cared, and life kept going.

I started going on really long walks for hours (because I no longer had hundreds of daily emails to sort through or a steady job to show up for). I began to notice that all the houses and driveways were empty Monday through Friday from 9:00 to 5:00. I found it interesting that all those people were grinding away somewhere that they, in all likelihood, didn't want to be in order to afford these nice houses and cars that they didn't have much time to enjoy. The neighborhood was a ghost town from 9:00 until 5:00, Monday through Friday. People were spending all this money and binding themselves to debt while they were spending all their time in service to that debt. The things they apparently most wanted were the things with which they were spending the least amount of time.

I began more frequently pondering the patterns of human beings. Todd Ballenger had introduced me to that concept—that all human beings are really just creatures of habits and patterns. I combined those thoughts with the idea that the exact opposite of my own habits and patterns was true. I was miserable over my pattern of being held hostage to an office and spending far less time than I wanted to on the things that truly mattered to me, and I wondered how I could flip it to the exact opposite reality—no longer in service to debt and spending the majority of my time in a location I loved with the people I loved.

I also began thinking about the "drone footage" of my life, and I started to view this life wherein Mike gets out of bed, brushes his teeth, and goes to the office. I thought, "What if I drew a line that illustrated my days?" And when I envisioned it, I was watching a line that did nothing but go back and forth to and from the office every day. I thought, "Fuck, that's boring." I began questioning why I was engaged in that pattern and in those habits when I really didn't like them! Why was I leaving my kids and my wife, who I wanted to spend more time with? Why was I sleeping for eight hours and then gone for ten, leaving myself with only a three- or four-hour window to spend time with my family? I found myself recognizing that, in my life, the reality should be the complete opposite.

When I envisioned that life—the one that sounded amazing—the line wasn't straight. It was all over the map. It made me think of the *Seinfeld* episode where George Costanza decided to do the opposite of what he'd always done. He kept getting results he didn't want, and Jerry suggested that he start doing the opposite of what he'd been doing. He started with lunch. Instead of ordering his usual tuna on rye, he ordered tuna salad, a croissant, and a hot tea with lemon. Some girl came up to him said, "You ordered the exact same lunch as me! I'm Victoria, hi." He got a new lunch *and* a girlfriend out of it.

It was time for me to start doing the opposite.

ENTREPRENEURIAL REALITY CHECK

*Deciding to be an entrepreneur is easy, but
being successful at it is not simple.*

Within a few months, a friend from my former mortgage company and I decided to create a nonprofit financial literacy website for high school kids. This was it, I would create a new business on my own terms. I thought, "This is easy. I'll just create this." After three weeks or so, I was in the zone. I truly believed I'd found my "thing."

I was studying like crazy and was still in Todd Ballenger's mentorship program when I got the idea. He asked if he could do a presentation on me in order to share my experience with the group since I'd just quit my job. I told everyone in the room what I was planning to do with the financial literacy business. The room was filled with people who had money to spend, and one guy said, "I want to support that. I can give you the money you need to get it off the ground." He gave us $100,000. We created a contract and were excited to have a little bit of runway. We found one other investor who also gave us about $100,000, and with that, we thought we had enough money to build the website and make our venture successful.

We began interviewing high school kids, and I travelled a bit to figure out how to fully develop the company. We ran out of money within five months exclusively through website development costs and paying ourselves. I was still living with the mindset that I needed to pay myself $10,000 per month; I clearly wasn't yet a true entrepreneur. Looking back now, I shake my head as to how naïve (and stupid) I was.

The loss of our investors' money on top of the previous challenges in that six-month period completely wrecked me. I felt so much shame around the belief that I'd just pissed away these people's hard-earned money—people who trusted me to do something impactful with it. It became painfully obvious that that particular business was not going to work, which meant I then had the unpleasant task of breaking it to my investors—once I was able to swallow the huge lump stuck in my throat. Thankfully, the investors were quite gracious, and I remember saying to them, "I don't know what I'm going to do, but whenever my life turns around and I have an abundance of money— because I'm not going to quit—I will pay you back." In hindsight, it's probably good that I had no idea it was going to take over a decade to do that.

Suddenly, there I was, in even more debt, which I hadn't thought was even possible. Did I mention that my wife had given birth to our daughter, Lucy, during this time? So, in addition to the stress of being the father of a newborn and a toddler as well as the sole supporter of our family, I went from being about $50,000 in debt to being $250,000 in debt (at least in my mind because I still owed our investors a return on their investments). I honestly didn't believe there was any chance I would ever be able to repay it. That was the feeling that overwhelmed me most. "I've created a monster, and no matter what I do, I will likely never be able to repay this."

Amazingly, this wasn't my ultimate bottoming-out point. It was certainly one of them, but I bounced a few times, the way Navy SEALs do during the exercise where they have their hands and feet tied together and then have to bounce off the floor of a pool to get to the surface and inhale before sinking right back down.

It was the point at which my ego was gone, my self-confidence and self-worth completely destroyed. I felt isolated, powerless, and confused as to what I should do next.

Which leads me back to that night my doorbell rang.

That burly, bearded, Paul Bunyan-channeling tow truck driver knocked on our door and asked for the keys to my car so that it could be repossessed by the bank. Honestly, if he didn't have a towing outfit on, he could easily have been wearing a plaid shirt and carrying an axe. I had a feeling that he was not only a tow truck driver but also a "repossession bouncer" of sorts—you know, about six-foot-two, 220 pounds, there not only to tow a car but also to intimidate someone into letting him do so without putting up much of a fight.

I made up a story about an agreement we'd "just made" with the bank. Because we were likely his last stop (with grease on his hands and face, he looked like he'd already towed several vehicles that day), he accepted our story. But he said that he was going to call the bank the next day, and if our story didn't check out, he would be back. And, if he came back, he was taking the car. I said to Katie that night, "Let's just leave it out front with the keys in it." We left that car in front of our house—with the keys in it—for three weeks. But to our astonishment, he didn't return to take our car.

TRYING TO ESCAPE

No matter how hard you try, it's impossible to
run away from yourself.

For the previous few years, we had casually tossed around the idea of moving to Seattle. The mortgage company had expanded into Washington, and we thought it might be fun for me to run a branch in Seattle where we could also spend more time near Katie's best friend and closer to her family. It was never a super serious discussion, until we got to a place where nothing was really holding us in Oregon, and I felt like I wanted to escape anyway. After the tow truck driver drove off, I thought, "You know, we've literally lost just about everything at this point." I had about $7,000 left, and I said, "Now's the time. Let's move."

I felt so much shame around Portland. I didn't want to go anywhere and risk running into anybody I knew. We drove up to Seattle a couple of weekends in a row and picked a house to rent—a house we never should have chosen because it was way more house than we needed or could pay for at the time. Much like when I was paying myself $10,000 per month even though our business was nowhere near profitable or stable, my mind was still a bit delusional in terms of what we needed, what we could truly afford, and how long it might be before we got back on our feet.

When we moved to Seattle, we drove there in our Mercedes. It was the same Mercedes that had sat in front of our house with the keys in it for three weeks, just waiting for the tow truck driver to return. During the drive, I told Katie that I could no longer have the guilt or the monthly payment for that car hanging over my head. It was too stressful. I had to do the right thing and give it back to the bank that owned it. I was determined to find a reliable car I could purchase for $4,000 or under.

I went to check out two different minivans for sale on Craigslist, and Katie would have killed me if I'd come home with the first one because it was absolutely disgusting. I was so turned off I almost didn't even bother to look at the second option, but something compelled me to give it a chance. I was so grateful I did because it was only $3,500 and was in far better condition than the first one.

I finished all the paperwork on our new Kia minivan, got the keys, and walked out of the dealership. I sat in the front seat of the Kia and called the bank right then and there. I said, "I'm no longer in Portland. I'm in Seattle. Here's the location of the car. I'll leave the keys in it, and you can have someone come and pick it up." And they did.

The crazy thing was, we quickly grew to love that minivan, much more than the Mercedes. It made getting around with a baby, a toddler, and a stroller a hell of a lot easier. Believe me, if my 25-year-old self had known I would one day be a family man who loved driving a minivan, I would have figured out how to travel to the future just to kick my own ass. But, as corny as it may sound, it was the beginning of learning to do what was best for our family and not care about how others perceived us, especially when it came to material things. It was a little bit of wisdom in the form of sliding passenger doors.

We stayed in our rental house for four months or so before we had to break the lease and move into an apartment that was more affordable. The universe was teaching me lessons repeatedly, and this turned out to be another one. The rental house was beautiful but huge—our kids wouldn't sleep in their rooms because they were too far away from our own. The apartment ended up being just right, and Katie made it feel like home. The kids loved living there so much more because they were always closer to us (and started sleeping in their own beds!), and Katie loved that there was less to clean. Our ideas of what we truly needed continued to evolve.

During that time, I did whatever I had to do to bring in enough money to pay the basic bills. My parents graciously helped us out by letting me borrow money to keep us afloat. I tried my best to shield Katie from the brutal reality of how little money we had left, but she could see the writing on the wall. She asked me several times if I thought she should get a job, but I had too much pride to say Yes. Our plan had always been for her to be a stay-at-home-mom. But she was fed up with feeling helpless. We had diapers to buy and tiny mouths to feed.

So she decided to ignore my protests and managed to get a job working nights as a bartender at a casino on an

Indian reservation. Not only would she be making a few dollars above minimum wage (plus tips), we would also be able to join their very affordable family health care plan. She began working a few weeks before Thanksgiving in 2008. The very first night she worked was during employee appreciation, so the free buffet meals provided to employees during their shifts included fresh cut prime rib. She felt so guilty on her first night, filling up a plate of food knowing we were at home with a pitifully empty refrigerator. They sent all employees home with a Thanksgiving turkey that week, and I would be lying if I said we didn't shed tears of gratitude.

In addition to securing a job, Katie also went online and applied for welfare—something my ego would not have been able to agree to had I known. She told me about it once the application process was complete and we had an in-office appointment we needed to attend. It's funny how you can think that you've reached your lowest possible point, and then something happens to drop you even lower. We were running late to the appointment (because babies don't care what's on your schedule; they eat and poop on theirs), so I was speeding through a residential area and got pulled over by the police. Yes, I am the guy who got a $200 speeding ticket on the way to the welfare office. Lucky for me, my wife has a pretty good sense of humor and managed to lighten the situation by saying, "One day we will look back and laugh at this, right?"

I was too embarrassed to even walk into that office. Katie knew it was something she had to handle alone, and she did it despite her own feelings of shame. Growing up poor, she was mortified that she found herself standing in a line she vowed never to be in. But reality doesn't give a shit about feelings, and her instinct to feed her babies was greater than the shame of asking for help. She walked out of that office having qualified for $550 a month in groceries that would be loaded onto a debit card within the week. In addition, because we had an infant and a toddler, we also qualified for monthly checks from WIC, which is the Women and Infant Children program that pays for specific items like formula and baby food.

Katie felt like she had won the lottery. She was so relieved to be able to go to the store and immediately get food to feed our kids. We both agreed that we would never forget the feeling of gratitude we had that day. Through lived experience, we understand how devastating a feeling it is to not be able to buy basic necessities for your family. Quite simply, it is both ego and soul crushing. Having the weight of providing food taken off of our shoulders at that time was huge.

I could not admit it at the time, but I felt relieved once we got used to Katie working. It took a tiny bit of stress off my plate as I continued to search for work myself. I felt like I was grasping at straws. I went onto eLance (now Upwork) and applied for nearly everything. I remember thinking, "I just ran a multi-million-dollar company with 250 employees, and I can't get a job." I quickly discovered how un-hirable I truly was. I was turned down for jobs left and right, including one that paid only $14 per hour. I applied to be a CEO's assistant, and I was turned down.

Two or three months after we moved to Seattle, completely exhausted from the odd jobs I was doing to make ends meet, I reached out to two guys who used to work for Alpine Mortgage when we were first expanding the business into Washington. We had a lunch meeting and I told them I was looking for some consulting work. They said they could help. They'd started their own business and still had a rosy vision of me as the guy who ran the company as the marketing and sales engine. They asked me to help them, so I took a job consulting for them for $4,000 per month. While I had a steady job, I was back in a 9-5 situation. Believe it or not, that was perhaps my lowest point because it gave me a sense of what it felt like to give up on your dreams, to quit and be forced to completely cave to the corporate bullshit I'd determinately left less than a year before. I'd believed I was going to make it work no matter what, and yet there I was, back in a suit and tie, back in a corporate office.

We rarely got to spend more than a few hours each week together as a family during this time. Katie left for work at 4:00pm and didn't get back home until almost 4:00am. We passed like ships for nearly eighteen months. She'd wake up just in time to take over with the kids' morning routine and for me to head to a coffee shop or the office of the mortgage company for which I'd begun consulting. The only day when we really spent time together was Sunday; we both took the day off and went to the local farmer's market and park as a family.

The whole scenario felt like a massive step back. I felt as though I'd completely sold out. I'd taken a paying job I was completely qualified for, but it wasn't what I really wanted. I related to Demi Moore's character in the movie *Indecent Proposal*; I did something I never wanted to do just for the money.

After consulting for them for five or six months, I wore shorts to the office one day. I wasn't concerned about what they thought; I was coming in to help them with their sales and advertising, and they had a living room-sized office. I later got an email from one of the owners saying that I needed to wear professional attire into the office from that point forward. Not only was I being told what to do again, but I was also being told what to wear? Hell No. (P.S. I still love both these guys to death, and I'm forever grateful that they gave me an opportunity when they did.)

After everything I had been through, you might ask yourself why in the world I couldn't just let it go, suck it up, and wear the suit and tie. Millions of people work jobs they hate just to make ends meet. I guess that, for me, the pain of forcing a square peg into a round hole was too much. I just could not fit into that mold, and it made me sick even to try. I knew Katie would support me (both literally and figuratively this time) as I tried to plan an escape. I decided to reach out to my friend Tom, who I'd known from Todd Ballenger's mentorship group.

Tom Griffith and I met on September 11, 2007 in Dallas. Our connection was strong from the beginning because we were both mortgage business owners, and both from Oregon. We stayed in touch after the mentorship group ended and we had done a little work together. After some conversation, we decided to start a company called Up and Automated, which would help businesses build their websites and automate their marketing efforts. That venture marked my entrance into the brand-creation space. It was now early 2010. One of our clients was a mortgage company, which was great because I understood that industry inside and out. We were able to sign them to a $4,000 per month retainer, so my earnings while switching over from the consulting gig to this didn't change much.

Within thirty days of receiving the email from the consulting firm's owner declaring that I had to wear a suit to the office, I quit and put all of my energy into Up and Automated. I made enough to survive, and Katie's income supported us over the next year until the lease on our apartment was nearing renewal, and we learned that they would be increasing our rent to an amount beyond our reach. By this point, Katie had been bartending for over a year and a half, and the late, long hours at the casino was wearing on her. We decided to explore other options.

My parents lived in Tigard, which is a suburb of Portland, but they also owned a house in Corvallis, which is about seventy-five miles south. Their plan was to move there once they retired. They occasionally rented it to visiting professors at Oregon State, but mostly it sat empty except for when they stayed there on weekends during the football and baseball seasons. We had visited several times as a family and always enjoyed being there. As we brainstormed ideas on what our next move could be, Katie tossed out the thought of asking if my parents would rent us their house; we could move down there. She has genius ideas that pop up out of nowhere sometimes, and this was such an occasion.

ARRIVING HOME AND THE DISCOVERY OF TRUE FREEDOM

Home is a state of mind. It's where you want to be with the people you love the most.

I had never considered it before, but suddenly, it made the most sense. I always enjoyed being in Corvallis, and we knew it would be a great place to settle down and raise our kids. To this day, my mom could tell you exactly where she was, what she was doing, and probably what she was wearing the day I made that call to her. She was so ecstatic at the thought of us living closer to them, and for her to be able to see her grandkids more often.

Sidenote: I think my mom, Joanne, is where I got my stubborn nature and commitment to seeing things through to the end. She worked for more than thirty years at Nike, while also somehow managing to run the family, organize trips, manage sports schedules, and make sure there was always a hot dinner ready at the end of every day. I'm still not sure how she got it all done.

Back to Corvallis. My parents agreed, and we settled on paying $1,000 rent per month. Tom, my business partner, said, "I'll give you 100% of our revenue to help out if you just move back." And just like that, we were packing up, ready to move on to the next big phase in our lives.

Once we got settled at the house in Corvallis, life seemed to come into balance again. Katie was back to being a stay-at-home mom, and we were happy she was no longer working late night hours. The house we rented from my parents had a garage attached to the front and also another small building in the back of the house called "The Studio." It had hardwood floors and heating and functioned perfectly as my new at-home office. I only had to walk down my driveway off of the back deck to get to work, and I could wear whatever I damn well pleased. The added bonus was anytime I needed to take a ten-minute coffee break or grab lunch, I got to walk into the house and see my wife and kids. We knew the Corvallis move was the right one.

As we settled into our new lives, my son Jeff started kindergarten. When spring rolled around, I wanted to put him in T-ball, and I also had the opportunity to be the coach of his team. It was a great experience; it created a balance for me between work and play times, and I was finally getting a taste of what that ideal lifestyle I'd been working toward could actually feel like. During the first few games, Katie started introducing herself to some of the other parents whose kids were on the team. We didn't have any friends in town (and we didn't make *any* in Seattle— not one) and she was determined to be a little more social. As any stay-at-home mom will tell you, it can be incredibly isolating, especially if you're in a new town where you don't know anyone. Through T-ball, we gained an amazing circle of friends. I went on to coach Jeff's baseball teams until he was in fifth grade. It was a great experience for both of us.

We'd driven the Kia minivan for the duration of our time in Seattle, but the year after our move back to Corvallis, it started breaking down all over the place. The door wasn't working properly, the turn signals weren't working, the list of issues went on and on. Before we moved back, in fact, Lucy (who was two and a half at the time) thought it was her own personal slot machine. She dumped about $50 in quarters into the vents over time, and every time we turned left or right, we'd hear the quarters swishing around in the guts of the car.

I told our friends in Corvallis that if one more thing went wrong with the car, I was selling it. A month or so later, a headlight went out. It would have cost a whopping $20 to fix, but I'd said, "The next time something breaks, I'm selling it," and by that point, I was absolutely walking my walk and talking my talk. I sold it that very day on Craigslist for $750. My friends were like, "Wow, you're legit! When you say you're going to do something, you follow through!"

Because that's who I had decided to be.

The Kia had become as much of a joke as the couch that we arrived in Seattle with (and left without). It was a nice couch—my parents gave it to us—but it was huge and extremely heavy. We were living in an apartment with a staircase that curved as it went immediately from the front door up to the first floor. It barely fit through the front door, and once we got it up to the family room, it slowly began to be destroyed. Kids destroy everything when they're that young, and this couch was no exception. It was drawn on with Crayons, written on in pen, and covered in spilled coffee and booze stains. It had also been scratched to death by Katie's cat, Sofie. This cat was so skittish that we dated for a year before I ever met her. I thought Katie was lying about having a cat to begin with! After a while, I felt like Sofie needed a friend, so I bought another cat. They didn't get along. So I did what any reasonable person would do: I bought another cat. The two I bought got along great, but Sofie never got along with either of them. The sofa was a disaster (as was the cat). I chose to duct tape the cushions together at one point in an effort to get just another few months out of it.

Once we made the decision to move to Corvallis, I told Katie that I was not taking that fucking thing with us (the sofa, not the cat). I didn't want to tell her precisely when I was getting rid of it in advance, and there was no way I could get it down the stairway and outside by myself. I realized that if I cut it into pieces, however, I could get it out of there. On our final night in Seattle, my parents had taken the kids back to Oregon, Katie went to work at the casino, and I drove down the hill to Home Depot and bought a $40 Sawxall. I took the cushions and pillows out to the dumpster and then just started sawing it apart. It wasn't long before I ran into the springs, which I hadn't thought about. For some reason, I was thinking the whole thing was made of wood. So I went back to Home Depot to buy wire cutters in order to cut through the springs. Once I had it in four manageable pieces, I lugged each piece to the dumpster. Katie came home the next morning and asked, "What did you do with the couch?" I told her I threw it away, and she asked how the fuck I got it downstairs. I told her. If you ask her about it even today, she'll roll her eyes.

Sofie the cat went missing the very day we moved back to Corvallis. She was 15 at the time, and we couldn't find her anywhere. Katie was completely devastated; she cried during most of the drive there. Exactly sixty-seven days after we arrived in Corvallis, we got an email from one of our old neighbors saying that she thought she saw Sofie. It was a Thursday, and I asked Katie if she wanted me to drive the six hours to Seattle to try to get her. I don't know why I even asked; of course she did. I hopped in the car and left. Halfway there I recognized that I was wearing shorts and a T-shirt, and it was the end of October in Seattle.

When I got there, I saw Sofie within the first half hour. She was sitting by a pool and bolted when I began to approach her. I waited, freezing, for an hour and a half for her to come back. Which she did. This time, I approached her more slowly. And again, she bolted. I had no idea how hard it is to catch a cat! I took a break and went to dinner at the casino where Katie had worked, said Hi to a few people, and warmed up. I then returned to the pool and Googled "How do you catch a cat?" According to Google, one does not catch a cat. You wait for it to come to you. Even if you're freezing in shorts and a T-shirt, it's dark out, and you're six hours from home.

I told Katie, "Now that I know she's alive and I've seen her, I'm not coming home without this cat." I sat there for two and a half hours, and for two of those hours, Sofie was forty feet in front of me. We had a two-hour long staring contest. She finally walked up to me at 2:00am. I grabbed her, and we began the drive back home.

I arrived home at 10:00 the next morning, and we left almost immediately for the Oregon State football game as though none of it had happened and Sophie had been with us the entire time. We enjoyed two more years with her before she passed away.

Over the next few years, we went through several life changes. My parents moved down to Corvallis to retire, so we moved out of their house and found a place to rent that was just the right size with a huge backyard for the kids. My daughter Lucy started school, and my wife began working for my dad at his pitching toe business.

I learned that true freedom isn't all about the money, and it's certainly not about accumulating stuff. It's about creating the ideal structure for you, your life, your work/life balance, your family, and your friends. Once you discover what that is for you and get there, nobody can take away your freedom.

My business continued to evolve as I figured out, one step at a time, how to achieve and sustain my ideal lifestyle. I moved on from my business partnerships and went out on my own. There have been ups and downs, lessons and triumphs, wins and losses, pivots and hard stops. And I'm grateful for every single one because they are what collectively created The Makeover Method™ and the book you're reading right now.

THE KNOWLEDGE, EXPERIENCE AND WISDOM THAT LED TO OVERNIGHT SUCCESS

There is a way to create the life and business of your dreams.

It wasn't until I was in the midst of writing this book that The Makeover Method™ became a living, breathing concept. I liken the method to a baseball team—every player is critical. Even if you remove only the first baseman, the rest of the team is going to struggle. A lot.

The reason the method is critical is that there is a domino effect when any one of its components is missing or unclear. Just as no position on a baseball team can be eliminated, no part of The Makeover Method™ can be eliminated. It starts and ends with the business owner being able to self-evaluate and regulate where he or she is, both professionally and personally.

My overnight success comes on the heels of a decade-long journey that included investments in excess of $200,000. It is the result of my combined knowledge, experiences, and ultimately, wisdom.

When I was running Alpine Mortgage, I had five partners. We collectively had strengths and weaknesses in almost the same areas, and somewhat surprisingly, this was a huge part of our downfall. The complexity of going from one owner to a partnership, or from two partners to three is much like having kids. It gets exponentially harder as you grow. Two to three partners is more like two to nine. If you're like my co-author, Elizabeth Lyons, and you have five kids (and two of them are twins), you might find yourself pulling your hair out from the stress of it all.

My first mentor, Todd Ballenger, used to say that partnerships are "the leakiest ship in the sea." If you're trying to develop a personal brand or a business and you're going to build it as a partnership, you'd better be rock-solid on your joint or collective vision and the roles each of you will play. You'd also better have people in the right seats on the bus in terms of strengths and weaknesses. Everyone has to have their confidence secure and be aware of his or her limiting beliefs. Everyone's strengths need to complement one another's, and everyone's weaknesses have to be accounted for so that it's clear who can pick up the slack when challenges arise.

Before you dive into The Makeover Method™, you need to be able to answer one simple question (that most can't answer): "What do you want?"

It will dramatically speed up the process if you have complete clarity around the ideal lifestyle you're trying to create for your life and business. Once you do that, the many obstacles and questions that you'll encounter along your journey will become much easier not only to ask but also to answer because you'll know exactly what you're striving to build. If you don't know what you're trying to create—if you don't know, for example, that you're trying to create a business where you can work whenever you want with whomever you want, and that you want massive amounts of money, no debt, and a small team so you can spend more time with your spouse and kids—you can get really confused really quickly.

And you'll stay that way.

In March 2008, I knew the details of my ideal lifestyle, even though I didn't know what industry I would end up in or how I would reach that vision at the time. I didn't have a specific company attached to it or a clear plan on how I was going to get there, but I knew what it looked and felt like. The biggest part of this challenge is determining what it is that you really want. Most people can't answer that question. They'll flounder for years around that it, delivering canned answers that they can't qualify with details. Once you can explicitly define what you want, you have to build an unwavering self-confidence that you can tap into no matter what obstacles you encounter. You have to stop telling yourself all the reasons you can't do it. Then and only then can you finally get to work on creating it.

Once I determined what my ideal lifestyle looked like, I had to break down that vision into tasks I could focus on and control each and every day. It's critical to say, "These are the three things I'm going to take action on today," and then commit to enjoying the process of completing them.

I've used virtual mentors I've never met in person, such as Gary Vaynerchuk, who once said, "It's not about buying the New York Jets. It's about loving the process of trying to buy the New York Jets." That really resonated: the idea of loving the process of working toward my ideal life. For a long time, I felt like I was constantly striving but never arriving, struggling through each and every task and to-do.

The shift for me lied in understanding that I'm improving and compounding that improvement every single day. It was also about recognizing that there is no "there" that I had to reach in order to be successful. There was no "right" there or "wrong" there. There was no magic fucking pot of gold at the end of the rainbow, as Mike Kemski says. It's about no longer focusing on getting to the end of the rainbow, and instead just enjoying each day.

I had to recognize that my ideal lifestyle was (and is) a slowly moving target, much like driving behind somebody in a dust storm. I was driving behind my brother one weekend last year as we drove to the river. There was so much dust in the air that I couldn't see more than five feet in front of me. We were both driving slowly enough that, as long as I stayed focus on his taillights, I knew I wouldn't lose him. We were on our way to the Bend Lava Caves with our kids for the first time, and once we were inside, we turned off all of our flashlights. It was so dark that you literally couldn't see your hand in front of your face. That's how it sometimes feels when you're in search of your ideal life. It's as though you know the target is close by, just as is your hand or the cavern walls in the darkness of the cave. You have a vision of it, you have a knowing that it's close, but when you get to where you thought the cave wall was, you recognize that what you were looking for is a few feet to the left. So you pivot.

Many of the obstacles you'll encounter will only appear after you are in motion, taking action in the market with your products and services. Your ideal outcome is the kind of moving target you can never squarely hit; it's more of a challenging but absolutely doable obstacle course. You can only see the obstacle ahead of you, and you go as hard as you can toward it. The rest of the obstacles are behind a wall; you can't see them. Once you complete the first obstacle, however, the wall opens up and the next obstacle becomes visible. You start to become better at focusing only on the next obstacle, not the next thirty-seven obstacles. You know that, by tackling one obstacle at a time, you will eventually beat the level, at which point the doors to the next level will open and amazing new opportunities will present themselves to you. It's not worth spending any mental energy on anything beyond the next obstacle, and continuously doing so represented a lack of confidence and trust on my part. Wanting to know how it was all going to play out was, at its core, a self-confidence issue. I had to learn to trust myself to take the most appropriate action each and every day. No matter what obstacle presented itself to me along the way, I knew I could figure it out and overcome it.

While your ideal outcome may be a slowly moving target, the most efficient way to most effectively hit it is to get your self-confidence to the point where you know—

beyond the shadow of a doubt—that you have the ability to hit whatever target you aspire to hit. You believe in your ability to engage in the process of finding it, aiming at it, and hitting it.

One practice that gives me peace is asking myself, "Did I do my best today?" When my head hits the pillow at the end of the day, did I waste the day? Did I spend four hours playing video games? Maybe I choose to do that on a specific day when I need a reprieve, but hitting my pillow at the end of the night and not having any regrets about how I spent my day is the goal.

Not even the greatest mentors can tell you what your goal *should* be. If you approach a guy like Russell Brunson or Tony Robbins and ask, "Should I write a book?" and that's his first interaction with you, he'll say (I hope), "I don't know enough about you to answer that question. I need to know what your mission is, what your plan is, what you're trying to create with your life." Good coaches and mentors will ask you a hundred questions before they'll ever give you an answer.

Regardless of what a guru or mentor ultimately advises, the key point is that there's no right or wrong answer when it comes to you. There's only the answer that gets you closer to your ideal lifestyle, one way or another. But, there is also an answer that will take you farther away from that ideal lifestyle. Sometimes, the only way to determine that is by taking action, testing your idea it in the marketplace, realizing it's taking you in the wrong direction, and pivoting (quickly).

Before I get into each step of The Makeover Method™, I'll share one story from my time in Dan Sullivan's

Strategic Coach program that helped me focus on all the right things.

I was in Santa Monica, CA for my first meeting and the coach in the front of the room starts the day with:

"At what age do you think you will die?"

Holy shit. I thought I was going to learn some stuff about becoming a better entrepreneur, and that's what you hit me with at eight in the morning?

Once we each chose an age, a magic wand was waved, and we were given extra years.

My chosen age at death was eighty-four, and when it was declared that I got extra years, I was asked how many extra years I wanted. I chose seven. I was then asked, "What do you want to do during the last seven years?"

I wrote down every single activity that came to my mind. We spent two or so hours on this exercise, and I noted everything I wanted to do: learn piano, learn Spanish, swim with dolphins, go to Italy, the list went on. We were then taught a time management system referred to as the "Entrepreneurial Time System" that freed up a lot of time—perhaps 150-175 days per year—wherein we'd do no work. Zip, zero, nada. The reason they had us create the list of things we would do in the bonus years we didn't know we'd get was so that we'd know what to fill that new "empty" time with.

I couldn't imagine what I'd gotten myself into. I hadn't taken more than a few days off per quarter, and these people wanted me to schedule my time off *first?* How was that going to work? I was there to grow my business, not plan my vacations! As it turned out, the Strategic Coach coaches know what they are doing, and they have consistent results to back it up. Their system forces you to build systems and a team because, as we all learn before long, none of us can do it all alone. That's part of the ideal lifestyle: creating time to focus on what we want to enjoy.

When you start out and say, "This is what my ideal lifestyle looks like. This is the star I'm going toward," you take wild swings like a brand-new golfer, sending the ball sailing to the left and the right in order to figure out the course. Each time you play, your deviations become far less dramatic. You get to a place where you know that it's most effective to use a 5-iron on the second shot of the tenth hole, and to aim to the left side of the green to leave yourself an uphill putt and avoid the bunker on the right.

My point is this: life is short, and you need to be clear about what you want and use your time wisely in order to achieve your ideal lifestyle.

THE MAKEOVER METHOD™

Life is short, and you need to be clear about what you want and use your time wisely in order to achieve your ideal lifestyle.

MADEOVER

In business, you get to a place where you recognize, "I'm not having three-hour catch-up coffee meetings with people anymore" or "letting people pick my brain when they feel like it." You get so damn clear on what actions and mindsets get you closer and which take you farther from your overall goal. An interesting byproduct of that honing of your daily routines, habits, and tendencies is that your clients also tend to fall into alignment with your approach. My clients today are all passionate about their area of expertise and have a zest for life. They want growth. They want to make a difference in their niche and leave a legacy. True impact.

Some of them may be a few steps ahead of me in terms of understanding certain aspects of their business and life, others are a few steps behind in certain areas, but they're focused on their ideal outcome, not micromanaging the work they've hired me to do. We all stay clearly in our own lanes. The more clarity you have on your ideal lifestyle and outcome, the more quickly and efficiently the entire puzzle comes together.

I share my stories, experiences, and The Makeover Method™ with one goal in mind that has nothing to do with me.

It's all about you.

The goal is to provide you with a systematic way of lessening the deviation from your ideal outcome, to speed things up for you and help you avoid the mistakes I've already made on your behalf. The more you can sort out your own mind and have clarity around where you're headed, the faster the wild swings go by the wayside.

Two years ago, I was so mentally overwhelmed from the moment I woke up to the moment I went to bed. All I could think about was, "How do I make this work?" Today, I have the answers for myself, and I want to share the key pieces of the puzzle that finally helped me get the life and business I used to only dream of.

Now it's your time, your turn to finally get the life and business you deserve.

Let's go.

THE MAKEOVER METHOD™

You don't have to figure it all out alone, there are others who've been there before that are willing to show you the way.

The remaining chapters of this book are dedicated to The Makeover Method™. It's the step-by-step process I went through to finally achieve the life and business of my dreams, the one that eluded me for an entire decade. This method not only worked for me but I've also proven it to work time and time again with clients I've coached through the process.

I'll share many of the stories from my personal journey and simplify each stage for you. There are countless resources and stories I chose not to include for your sake as the reader. I've chosen instead to expand upon each chapter and provide you with all of the resources that worked for me on my website.

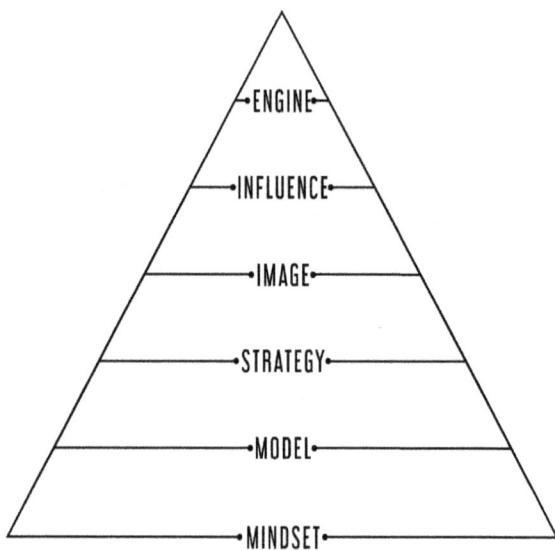

ENGINE

INFLUENCE

IMAGE

STRATEGY

MODEL

MINDSET

THE MAKEOVER MINDSET™

The missing link for so many years was in the five and a half inches in between my ears.

The combination of my mortgage company failure and my first entrepreneurial failure in 2008 took everything from me. Those back-to-back experiences not only stripped away all of my assets but also my self-confidence and self-worth right along with it. This led me to some of my darkest and loneliest days as an entrepreneur. Between 2010 and 2012, I did everything I could to avoid interacting with people and became fairly reclusive. I removed myself from all social media, hung out with only my wife and kids with very few exceptions, and made no attempts to develop friendships while we lived in Seattle. I knew at the most basic level that my self-confidence was fucked up because I wasn't functioning normally in social situations. At family dinners, I'd eat last. Or, everybody would have dessert and I would rob myself of it. I literally didn't think I was worth it. Or, more to the point, I thought everyone else was more deserving than I was.

I went through what I describe as my "self-discovery" phase as an entrepreneur. I began taking every online course I could get my hands on to learn marketing, advertising, and other details of how to run an online business. As I mentioned, I also partnered with a great sales person and idea guy, Tom Griffith. Through our company, Up and Automated, we created 50+ brands between 2010 and 2015, and I reinvested almost all of my earnings back into the business. We created a logo, social media presence, and website around anything we thought we could sell, and then pitched the idea to the market to see if it worked. Most of our ideas flopped, but three of them took off and had a very nice run of success, especially between 2012 and 2015.

I thought I was back.

It was a productive and creative way to hide my shame and guilt stemming from the failures of 2008 and 2009, but that's what it was: I was hiding behind the scenes as the Number Two guy, and I could feel a calling to go out on my own again.

BEGINNING THE AGENCY AND MY BREAKING POINT

By 2015, after creating so many brands and seeing what worked and what didn't, I knew I'd discovered my passion. My lead graphic designer had been with me full-time for over a year, and it was time for us to venture out on our own and begin helping others avoid many of the mistakes I'd made.

We called the company Your Branding Spot and began creating logos, a social media presence, and websites for our clients, and we did a lot of them from 2015-2017. Our team, skills, systems, and delivery all improved during those first two years. I was working my ass off and continuing to invest in my self-growth and online learning. By the end of 2017, I'd invested multiple six figures into online courses, events, and travel to discover the secret to running a proven and profitable business online.

But there was a glaring problem: I was still far from my ideal lifestyle and had, in a way, created my own living hell. My business was still not profitable. I was barely paying myself, and I worked 340 out of 365 days in 2017. Many days, I woke up early and worked, took my kids to school, worked a normal 8-4 day, took my kids to their sports practices, had family dinner, and then headed back to the office until midnight or 1:00am.

By October 2017, I was burned out, frustrated, broke, confused, and had begun arguing with my wife over finances. We rarely argue, but my grind and commitment toward the ultimate freedom and my ideal lifestyle was taking its toll on us all.

Something had to change.

THE BREAKDOWN THAT LED ME TO BREAK THROUGH

It was the wee hours of the morning, and Katie was sleeping next to me. I couldn't sleep. I was completely broken and frustrated. I remembered that scene from *Jerry Maguire* where Jerry has a mental breakdown and writes down his mission statement in an enlightened, all-night frenzy.

I was right where he was, about to completely lose my shit after investing so much, working so hard for so long, and *still* being broke as hell. It was almost 2:00am, and I was studying the work of the founder of ClickFunnels, Russell Brunson, when I ran across someone who had successfully implemented his methodology and software— Garrett White.

Garrett's documentary found me at just the right time. His core message was to stop fucking lying to yourself, tell yourself the truth, and take ownership of your life again in all areas, as a man. I had seen Garrett on stage in 2007 at Steven Marshall's event. He was a great speaker and ran a mortgage company at the time too. I learned that he had gone through a similar process of losing it all, and he had made it through to the other side. He'd found his ideal lifestyle again and put all of his knowledge and systems into a book, *The Warrior Book*. His message really resonated with me, and he seemed to have the answers to getting the life I was after. His book was a whopping $100. I remember thinking, *Shit, it must be good.* I quickly checked my bank and said, "Fuck it. I have $120 in the bank, and I'm going to spend $100 of it on this book and see what happens. Maybe this is the answer."

In a weird way, the book thoroughly helped me face some of my deep-seated self-confidence issues attached to the mortgage business, entrepreneurial ventures, and even not having made it in professional baseball. Garrett has a method and a system wherein he's very clear about what needs to be done first, second, and third. He has names for each phase, and I went through his book, which is essentially a manual for how you get what he refers to as a Core 4 lifestyle. The way the book is written helped me to understand that, as men, we've gotten to a place where, if you step back and look at the last three generations, it becomes apparent where we are and why. It helped me to see the bigger picture instead of being self-centered and having the sole perspective that my life wasn't working. It showed me how to think about things from a larger vantage point and then figure out a way that I could get everything I wanted out of life. Garrett developed a system, and he was prepared to show anyone ready to pay attention how to follow what he'd already done. The first step was to get extremely raw and real in a place he calls The Pit. It's basically a true assessment of where you *really* are today. You have to be 100% truthful with yourself about where you are with your body, being, balance, and business.

Part of that acknowledgement on my part started me down a path of consistent daily workouts, meditation, and journaling. I spent the first few days assessing my life, getting clear on where I really was. From there, it was important to assess where I wanted to be and determine the steps I had to take every single day in order to get from Point A to Point B. Going into The Pit was about truly assessing where I was, how I got there, what I wasn't happy about, what wasn't working, and—most importantly—why. Within the first week of reading his book, I found myself asking myself a lot of hard questions: "Why am I broke?" "Why am I unhappy?" I then asked the deeper psychological questions such as, 'If I'm drinking and smoking pot, that means I'm trying to escape some something. What am I trying to escape, and why?"

As they say, "When the student is ready, the teacher appears." Garrett appeared as the teacher at the perfect time for me.

Just ninety days later, I was a completely new man, but I continued to struggle financially with the business. knew I still needed help.

A LONELY SATURDAY
AND REACHING OUT FOR HELP

In January 2017, I met Mike Tietje in a digital marketing group, and we became fast friends. He'd been a US Marine for ten years with a background in human intelligence extraction, and he'd run over $60 million in traffic between Google AdWords and Facebook Ads. He began mentoring and coaching me through marketing, advertising, and copywriting. By June, he felt that my last true hurdle to get my business rolling was to step up my game with copywriting. He suggested that I start virtually following Mitch Miller in June 2017.

By January 2018, I'd been following Mitch for over six months, and I was still working almost every day trying to turn my business around. It was Saturday, January 6th, and I was going to spend the entire day in my office planning out my next moves with the business. I logged in to my computer and Mitch was doing a Facebook Live video from Phuket, Thailand. He called it "Your Freedom War Plan: Money | Travel | Business." It was like he was talking directly to me for over sixty minutes, and near the very end of the video, he said, "I'm surprised at how many people don't ask for help when they are stuck. Some people just need to ask for help." At that point, I was at my absolute rock bottom. I know I talked earlier on about hitting the bottom of the pool several times and bouncing back up to the top. But, at this point, I was unable to bounce back up again. I was not only financially falling apart; I feared I might actually end up divorced. Katie and I had begun arguing on a regular basis. They were little arguments about a variety of things, but really, at its core, it was about me spending all my time at the office while at the same time not making enough money. My parents were also starting to get extremely frustrated because they'd been helping us out so much financially. I was about to implode. I'd already imploded financially, so that part couldn't get any worse, but I felt like I was about to end up both financially wrecked *and* single without any semblance of a working business model to move forward with.

So, I did it.

I asked for help in a comment on one of Mitch's posts about eight days later. I said something like, "I just watched your Facebook Live last week, the one where you said that most people don't ask for help. I feel like I'm that guy. I need help. I've been at this for a decade. I haven't made any money, and I'm frustrated. I've put in the work, and I don't know where to turn or what to do, but I know I can't figure it out on my own."

Andrew Mercier, who was on Mitch's team at the time, commented almost immediately. "Get here and learn ten years' worth of knowledge in three days." He included a link to Project Persuasion 2.0, their event in Phuket,

Thailand. Right after that, Paul Halme commented, saying, "Project Persuasion is a total game changer."

I clicked the link. Holy shit. Yeah, right. The event was in Phuket, Thailand, 7,976 miles from my house—and only fifteen days away.

I responded with, "Fifteen days' notice might be tough," or some comparably bullshit answer. The truth was, I couldn't see any way to make it happen financially, the timing sucked, and how the hell would I explain it to Katie?

Two hours later, I was leaving my office to pick up my son from Parkour practice. Mitch himself sent me a private voice message and said, "Dude, I think you're a legit guy, and if you find a way to get here, I'll help you." I was ecstatic—and then immediately and absolutely terrified to tell Katie.

First of all, Katie and I have always been like college roommates in the sense that we're great friends who joke with each other all the time. We have a great relationship, and we might bicker every once in a while, but we don't fight. But I hadn't talked with her for two straight days. It was literally the longest fight we'd ever had as a couple. This wasn't terribly convenient given that I absolutely needed to talk to Katie about the trip…and we weren't talking.

While waiting in the parking lot to pick up my son, I checked to see if there was any possible way to move money around and actually afford a flight to Phuket and the fee to attend the event. After a little Expedia and bank research, I determined that I had just enough to do it. If I moved all my money from three separate places into one checking account, I could afford the flight. I didn't have enough money for food or the hotel (yet), and decided I'd figure that out later. I felt crazy, but what did I really have to lose?

I texted Katie and said, "You've got to calm down because I want and need to talk to you, and I'm not going to talk to you if you're pissed."

An hour later, I was home and sat down with her. I said, "I'm sorry that we're not getting along, but I need to talk to you about something." For the record, this is a notoriously bad way to start a conversation, and it's possible that she was waiting for an "I cheated on you" revelation.

She agreed to listen.

I told her that I had an opportunity that was going to sound crazy considering our financial status, but I thought I needed to go. Also, it was in Thailand. Also, it was in two weeks.

She paused for what felt like forever, but it was probably only five seconds before saying, "I think you've got to go." I said Okay, and five minutes later I logged on to Expedia and booked my flight. That period in time was one of the most awkward of my life. My relationship with Katie was fragile because our money had been so tight, and my relationship with my parents was fragile because our money had been so tight. My parents had been so graciously helping us, and I recognized that I was going to have to tell them that I was hopping on a flight to Thailand. It's a bit weird, to say the least, to be forty-four years old and worried about telling your parents something like that.

But I had to go. My life almost literally depended on it. I was at the point where I was starting to think, "Maybe this isn't going to happen for me. Maybe I should just go get a real job." I remember Katie saying something to the effect of, "If you don't do this, I'm worried about living with the person that you're going to become over the next thirty years. You will be a bitter man who quit on his dream." She knew that, if I didn't see this through after all that work I'd done over the previous decade, the death of me as a person would actually be much worse for her than it would be for me. I attached significant meaning to the concept of quitting. Most of all, I believed it would show my kids that it's okay to live a settled life instead of the life of their dreams. I would have utterly failed by settling and showing my kids that was just plain unacceptable to me.

Tony Robbins says that when people get to a place where they are really and truly ready for change, it usually comes from one of two possible sources: you know you're extremely broken (pain), or you know you have a passionate vision toward which you're so driven that you choose to make changes (pleasure).

I fit both categories.

PROJECT PERSUASION AND THE HOT SEAT

My trip from Corvallis, Oregon to the Opposed Media Compound in Phuket, Thailand took forty-seven hours. I bought the cheapest possible ticket, and it therefore had a couple of lengthy layovers in both Los Angeles and Singapore.

I went up to the mansion to meet the team: Andrew, Mac, and Mitch. We had a beer and a short chat before Mitch offered to take me down the hill to my hotel on his motorcycle. He said it was cool that I made the trip, asked me about some of my goals, and promised me that the next few days would change my life.

The first day of Project Persuasion was filled some mind-blowing knowledge in the areas of psychology and persuasion. This was not your normal event. The second day included a Hot Seat session, and the person in that Hot Seat was me.

I sat in the front of the room with Mitch. He took a breath and closed his eyes for a second. I later learned that before engaging in this exercise, Mitch clears his mind of all judgment, of everything he knows about marketing and psychology, and of all his opinions about how people should be running their business. He starts with a blank slate and simply listens. There were fifty or so people in the room as well as eight experts sitting in the front row. Everyone intently listened as I told the story of where I'd been, where I was, and how unsure and terrified I was of where I was going. I started getting choked up and said, "I've taken all the courses and worked my ass off. I'm just ready, you know?" I was almost to the point of tears when Mitch looked at me and said, "I think you *are* ready." He paused and then added, "And here's the good news: my team and I are going to help you. We're going to come in and help you turn this thing around."

He then began asking other experts what they thought and what they'd do with my situation. Macaully Ryan said he didn't get my offer at all. Jan Jagen, another member of the Opposed Media team said, "I'd create a high-ticket package and sell it through a webinar." Desislave Dobreva, who was one of the speakers at the event, said "I can help you with your brand strategy." Erica Blair, a brand strategist who also lives in Thailand, boldly said, "I think you have some real self-confidence issues. Your body language is very closed off." She suggested that I had a deeper issue to solve before I could solve any of the business-related issues. She approached me after the session and said she wanted to introduce me to her friend, Clay Moffat.

THE WIZARD WHO
CHANGED MY MINDSET

The next day, Erica and a stranger approached me. She said, "Mike, I'd like you to meet my friend, Clay Moffat." Clay said that he'd heard my story and would like to help me if I was open to it. I remember feeling like Jim Carrey in the movie *Yes Man*. People were offering to help me, and I was ready for the help. If someone offered to help, I said Yes.

Since it was the last day of the event, Clay said I should come to his place the next day so he could begin working with me. I said Sure, and we swapped numbers. We agreed to meet at 10:00am the next morning, and the plan was for me to meet with him and then go back and meet with Mitch and his team to start working on my execution plan.

The next morning, I jumped in a cab and headed to Clay's house. He lives in Chalong, which is about thirty minutes from Mitch's house. It's a really cool area full of

Muay Thai fighting gyms, massage clinics, and health food restaurants. It's like a street in the middle of Thailand dedicated to athletes and health-conscious individuals. In one hour, I saw no fewer than fifty people with six-pack abs just walking down the street. Everybody's there training to be an MMA or Muay Thai fighter. So I'm in the cab, thinking, "What the fuck am I doing with my life?" That's truly how I felt, and it's also how I felt on the flight over. But I was down for whatever was offered at that point. I didn't have much money going over, so every expense was a stretch, including the cab ride to Clay's.

When I arrived, we chatted for a few minutes, and he gave me a bit more background on his work. He's done a lot of work with NLP and hypnotism, and he stressed that his process works far better when his clients trust him. The night before, a group of us were having a beer on Mitch's back deck, and one of the other participants said, "You should stop drinking if you're meeting with Clay tomorrow." That's when I first learned that he was a mind conditioning expert and hypnotist and that I'd said Yes to something without really knowing what I was saying Yes to! He said, "If he's gonna hypnotize you tomorrow…" and my response was, "*What?*" Anyway, he said it works best if you haven't been drinking.

So I stopped drinking.

Clay told me that everything he does is designed only to help his clients get what they want. I told him that I trusted him, that I wouldn't be there if I didn't. I just really wanted the help. We sat down on what was basically the stereotypical therapist's couch. The day before, I'd taken about an hour to fill out a questionnaire for him, providing details about what was going on in my life and what I was feeling. He said he first needed to make sure that I could be hypnotized, so he did this exercise where he had me close my eyes and he told me to imagine that one hand had a weight on it and the other had balloons tied to it. He was speaking in a somewhat odd voice, and by the time I opened my eyes, my hands were about two feet apart, vertically. He told me he wanted me to keep my hands level, and yet by the time I opened my eyes, one hand was positioned two feet higher than the other. Apparently, that meant that I could be hypnotized. So that was good.

He asked me to close my eyes and had me walk down some steps in my mind while counting down from ten. In total, it felt like my eyes were closed for ten or fifteen minutes, but it had actually been an hour. He said we were finished for the day, and at that point I didn't feel like anything terribly significant had occurred. While I was "under," I was still aware of the room around me. I could still hear sounds, and I remember hearing people coming in and out of the house at one point. When you're under hypnosis, it's not like you're asleep or completely unaware of your surroundings, but I was definitely in a trance of some sort.

Before I left, Clay said that, essentially, he had set some foundational stuff in place so that when I went back home, he would be able to hypnotize me virtually. We planned to meet every week until the results we were pursuing had been achieved. That process ended up taking eight weeks for me, at which point I felt solid enough to stop the weekly hypnosis and continue with some of Clay's online daily conditioning programs and routines. I felt ready in every way.

I know you might be at a point where you're thinking, "Okay, so this is the part of Mike's story I can't identify with. This is the part where he got 'lucky' by meeting Mitch, the team of experts and Clay." I thought that too—for a bit. In fact, at several points during the event, I said to various people, "I can't believe how lucky am I that almost every one of the experts here has offered to help me." And every one of the attendees had the same response: "You're not lucky at all. You reached out to Mitch. You hopped on a flight. You made the decision when you did." A few of my friends back home said, "I don't think I would have reached out to Mitch. And if I did, I *know* I wouldn't have bought the plane ticket to go to Thailand, and I certainly wouldn't have done the hot seat. You earned this."

They were right. I'd done the work. I'd been kicked down over and over again. And I got back every single time. Even when I met Mitch, he didn't do the work for me. He handed me nothing on a platter. Hell, he barely handed me the platter. But he did offer it to me. That first night after I returned to my hotel, Katie called to see how the day had gone, and I was so choked up I couldn't even talk for several minutes. I finally said, "These guys are going to help me." The next six months would be the some of the hardest and most uncomfortable I'd ever experienced. Right around the ninety-day mark after going to Thailand was when the even more challenging work began. That was the point when, for the first time in my life, I started saying with great conviction, "Maybe I'm not talented enough. Maybe I'm not good enough." Just like in the hero's journey, I wondered, "Do I have what it takes?"

I wondered if, perhaps, I'd reached the end. Not in the sense that I considered ending my life, but there were a few times when I thought, "Maybe this whole thing truly isn't going to work." I used to joke with Katie (though I was semi-serious) that perhaps I should just go work at a car wash or mow golf course grass and at least be happy with my life making $7 an hour instead of grinding and continuing to try to figure it all out. There had been lots of hard times during the previous decade, no doubt. Mitch never told me that it would take at least ninety days to get some consistency, but for some reason, my mind was tied to ninety days. So, at the ninety-day point, when I still hadn't realized strong, consistent success, I thought, "It's been a decade. Maybe I'm just not good enough."

By this point, I'd taken several confidence courses and read a few books by people like Mike Kemski, Brené Brown, and Mitch Miller. Clay had also hypnotized me seven or eight times during those first few months, and he said, "Now we need to work on your sales calls." He started role-playing a sales call with me, and I don't know if he did it intentionally, but he was really hard on me. He really pushed me. Every time I flubbed a word, he almost purposely interrupted me to yell at me.

"Not fucking good enough, Mike," he'd say. "You're trying to sell a several-thousand-dollar package, and your confidence isn't there." We'd start again, and I'd get the same response: "Not fucking good enough." The third time, I got through the intro better, and then he hammered me on something—I don't remember exactly what it—but it was the third or so time in a row that he was borderline yelling at me about how badly I was doing. He basically said, "This is terrible. I'll never buy from you," and I just started crying. Here we were, in the middle of a Zoom session, and I was bawling to another grown man. I was so embarrassed, but he just said, "Hey, it's okay. Take a break. Don't give up."

That was a hard day. That was the day I continued to hear my own words of defeat echoing back to me. We all make up stories about how good or talented we are or aren't, but this guy, who I trusted, was giving me feedback that was really bad. I thought, I've put in ten years of work plus been hypnotized plus gone through this intense sales training, and I've got quite possibly another 100 days to get through. I've consumed everything Russell Brunson ever created plus Garrett White's book, and then I went to Mitch's event. I really thought this might take just one more big push. Just like having a baby (or so they say).

I was still working 24/7. I was completely physically and mentally drained, and then Clay pressed me on that day, and it just felt like, after all that work, somebody was telling me that I didn't have what it would take. The root issue was undeniably my mindset. My self-confidence issues, negative self-talk, and limiting beliefs were tough to break.

But then it happened.

I sold a brand makeover package. It wasn't to a friend or even a friend of a friend. It was a completely cold lead. In that moment, a light bulb went on. I realized, "This is actually possible. I was able to close a $7,800 sale." And then I got another lead who was local and wanted to meet face-to-face. I still felt relatively awkward and uncomfortable in social situations, and I was going to have to look another human being in the eye and confidently close a $7,800 sale. It was terrifying. But I closed it, and I remember driving back to my office with a cartoon-like smile on my face thinking, "Fuck, I've got this." That client later told me that I'd changed his business and life forever with what he learned from me through his experience. It was a significant moment for me because I'd felt the same way only months earlier about Mitch and his team.

Over the next sixty days, I'd experience the feeling of a $7800 sale another six times, and I was on my way to becoming The Makeover Master. It was time for me to build my systems, and my prices were about to go up.

I realize now that nobody can give you your life back. There's no luck. Nobody gifted me anything. I earned it all—all of the coaching and all of the mentorship. And then it was my responsibility to take it and do something with it. Mitch just showed me where the lock was that was keeping the one critical box in my experience closed: the box that held hostage my self-confidence and inability to let go of my limiting beliefs. He showed me where the key was, but not how to unlock the box. I had to do that part myself.

THE MAKEOVER MODEL™

The market is the ultimate judge and jury for your business idea, and it's always right.

The first "business-specific" step of The Makeover Method™ is proving your business model, which is extremely uncomfortable for most people. Because it's so uncomfortable, they either overthink it and never get started, spend only one day on it, or blow right past it.

Here's how you get out there quickly and effectively: make your best guess on your product or service and put it out to the marketplace to see how the market reacts. That's it. Then, get feedback and make changes as necessary. Once you get to the place where people are consistently buying from you, leaving positive reviews, and referring you to others, you've proven your business model.

THE MAKEOVER METHOD™

Make your best guess on your product or service, and put it out to the marketplace to see how the market reacts.

MADEOVER

While the combination of building self-confidence and eliminating limiting beliefs is the most underrated and under-discussed step in building your brand, proving your business model is the hardest part of the business side of the equation. Proving your business model comes with this degree of challenge because the only way to do it is to put your offer out into the marketplace and see how prospects react.

You can sit in a room for years, planning out every single funnel, tagline, and piece of ad copy only to finally implement and have the marketplace immediately tell you that it doesn't like the result of your five years of planning. Alternately, you can plan for five minutes and put it out there, prepared to get knocked down a few times. Todd Ballenger said something that stuck with me: "The market is always right. The only way to prove your business model is to put it out to the market, let it beat you down a million times, and tell you how wrong you are until you've gotten it right." You get kicked and kicked and kicked some more, and then, one day, you change or subtly tweak one or two things in your language or your package and "all of a sudden," it starts working. At which point, you're left wondering, How the hell did that happen?

I'm often asked how far out one has to think when proving their business model before executing it. It's essentially been proven that human beings shouldn't plan anything more than ninety days in advance. The human brain functions in such a way that any time period further away than that doesn't feel real to us. Once you know what you're selling and who you're selling to as well as have consistent sales—and the end result of those sales is that people either want to refer you out or leave you a positive review—it's time to blow up your reach and begin letting the masses know you exist. The business model will evolve and change in perpetuity, especially if you're like me, always looking for ways to improve and make more impact. Your price will increase, your package will become more exclusive, and your timeframes will expand.

The only way to prove your business model is to have the courage to put yourself out there and see what the marketplace reaction is. Just like fishing, you have to throw out the line and wait for the bite. If you never get a bite, you switch bait. Or locations.

I knew what my ideal lifestyle looked like, and while I didn't necessarily attach it to a specific business model, I knew that, at a super high level, I wanted few-to-no meetings, fewer phone calls, and lots of money. If you're stubborn and you say, "My package is $97 no matter what, and it's automated, and it's based off a shitload of landing pages and lead magnets," you can easily get into a pattern of not listening to the marketplace and staying stuck there for a very long time simply because you're determined to do it the way you initially decided you'd do it. The next thing you know, you'll have spent two and a half years tweaking everything, and it's being seen by a whopping sixty-four people per month.

Entrepreneurs who are too rigid about what their "thing" is going to be can go down a slow road to insanity. Find a hot market that interests you, find out what people in it want, and give it to them. That's the simplest and fastest way to make money with your business. I know what people want in the industry that I've attached myself to. We give it to them, and they are happy to pay us a premium for it because we are damn good at what we do.

When you begin to put your ideas out there, the first one hundred days of intentional execution can be really tough, and it's when most people get frustrated and quit. You have to be ready to make tweaks. I must have made a hundred little changes to our products, services, and the overall delivery of our makeover experience before we got it just right and changed our company name to "The Makeover Master" in 2018.

STAY FOCUSED ON YOUR IDEAL LIFESTYLE

While you are proving your business model, it's critical to remember why you are doing all of this in the first place. If you lose sight of that and begin changing things just to make money (like I did from 2012–2015), you'll end up with some money in your pocket, but you won't be happy. To achieve everything you want, you need to make decisions that are in alignment with selling more of your products and services, yes, but if it keeps you locked in an office eighteen hours a day, you'll be miserable.

My focus was always on design and branding, and I kept tweaking our process based on feedback from customers. There were plenty of times when I could have made more money faster in the process, but it wouldn't have provided me with my ideal lifestyle. I was willing to delay the financial gain as I put it all together.

While I'm glad I did, that doesn't mean it was always easy.

I remember one large corporate client that could have brought us a ton of income, fast. But they said they wanted to have twelve meetings over three months before signing a contract—in other words, before we would see $1. I remember checking my gut and almost immediately saying to them, "You know, I'm not going to do that; I don't think this will be a good fit." They were shocked, I honestly don't think anyone had turned them down before. But that level of bureaucracy would have driven me mad. I'd lived in that corporate environment once; I was not going to do it again. Simplicity and balance were critical to me. The bottom line was, I wanted freedom. I even got that word tattooed on my forearm. Meetings, phone calls, and emails are had, taken, and read by choice. If I want to work from Sun River one day while hanging out on the river with my family, I'm going to do that. If I want to work from New Zealand, Colombia, or Thailand, I can do that too.

THE FIRST 100 DAYS PROVING MY BUSINESS MODEL

For a long time, I was afraid to put myself out into the marketplace. I consistently butted heads with myself by declaring that my ideal lifestyle included doing my own thing, yet I hadn't built up my confidence enough to actually do my own thing! Further, the small semblance of self-confidence I did have was attached to Tom, my business partner. I knew I wanted no partners going forward, but for almost six full years, what I said I wanted and the way I was approaching business each day were out of congruence. For the first two years, I was doing my own thing, but I was going broke. I attached to Tom because I was tired and broke, and then I spent six years out of alignment because I said I didn't want partners, but I'd attached myself to a partner! Thankfully, he took advantage of an opportunity that came his way, and it forced me to actually live the existence I was claiming I so badly wanted.

The day when I recognized that a lack of confidence and an abundance of limiting beliefs were my main problems was February 2, 2018. For the next eight weeks, I took massive action. I went to Thailand to meet with Mitch. I went through all of Jan Jagen's sales trainings and his Client Hook system. And I worked with Clay Moffat for eight weeks. It took about one hundred days in total before I truly proved my business model. During those one hundred days, I had some sales, but they weren't in alignment with my ideal lifestyle. It was the toughest fucking one hundred days of my life, but it was absolutely worth it for the end result. Just before the one—hundred-day mark, I closed a local deal (the face-to-face meeting that terrified me), then I closed another one right behind it, and then I closed six more over the next sixty days. The mindblower was that, on Day 100, I made my first sale that was in alignment with my ideal lifestyle. It was the cementing factor of my newly established self-confidence, and the final nail in the coffin that held my old limiting beliefs. I knew I'd proven the business model, but there was still a tiny bit of doubt floating around in my mind—until the first payment hit my checking account. I remember driving home from a meeting, seeing that, and declaring out loud, "Fuck yeah. I've fucking got this." I was so fired up.

Right after I closed the face-to-face sale, I wondered for a brief time whether or not I could repeat it, but within a week, I got the second sale. Then it felt like, "Game on." I did hit a three- or four-week period with no sales, and I'll be honest, the doubt did slowly creep in. But then I got another sale. The story continues to develop, but I know in my core that my model is proven, my self-confidence issues are resolved, my limiting beliefs are gone, and my prices continue to go up while The Makeover Master is in high demand.

CREATING YOUR IDEAL MARKET VERSUS INVENTING A MARKET

You don't have to invent a market or something entirely new. So many entrepreneurs think that their idea has to be unique or revolutionary. It doesn't. It just has to combine your skills, knowledge, and talent with your ideal work and time structure. Do that, and you'll have created your ideal lifestyle without inventing anything or coming up with the next big thing.

THE MAKEOVER METHOD™

Combine your skills, knowledge, and talent with your ideal work and time structure.

MADEOVER

I didn't invent graphic design or the idea of building websites. There are hundreds of thousands of individuals and firms that can do that for you. I created a unique brand makeover experience via a process that took all of my knowledge and skills and combined them with my team's knowledge and skills as well as the way we uniquely package and deliver everything. We change people's lives and businesses with what we do, and the clients who invest with us reap the rewards.

When the housing market crashed, there was a book I read called *Fooled by Randomness* by Nassim Nicholas Taleb. It basically suggested that, while we think we're in control of certain things, the market is always truly in control. For a long time, I had a great sense of discomfort about the fact that I wasn't in control of the housing market. It was going to do what it was going to do with or without me.

It's critical to manage that discomfort without allowing fear to completely take over. One thing that I've done over the last ten years is develop my own "blue ocean" that can never be taken away. There's always going to be a business that's doing well and ready to level-up their brand. Even in times of recession, there's always someone who's killing it and ready to upgrade their brand. I've built The Makeover Master brand around my unique process and unique spin. I've created my business model around an industry and a business that no one can take away from me.

I'm no longer uneasy about my lack of control over the market from the standpoint that I can admit that I have no control over it. The only thing I have control over as a citizen is my right to vote. Or run for office, and there's no way I'd do that. The skeletons that would come out of the closet would be disastrous. But, I admit that I have no control over the macro side of the market. People want to complain over the dumbest shit, like the notion that technology's ruining our kids. There are young people today who literally take twenty-seven selfies to get the lighting right before they post to Instagram. And when they do post, if they don't get fourteen likes in the first fourteen seconds, they remove the post because they want it perfect. Those are the types of things over which we have no control; it's what human beings are doing on a mass scale. Recognizing that I have no control over it eased my anxiety.

Additionally, when I was in the mortgage industry, I was tied to one specific product in one specific industry. In many ways, I still am tied to one product, but the fact is that the main cause of my downfall wasn't a result of my lack of control over the industry. The main issue was that I wasn't good enough or smart enough at that time to figure out the solution. There are plenty of people who made it through the housing crisis. Plenty of people were still underwriting mortgages and doing well. I couldn't figure it out at the time. I didn't have the skill set, knowledge, and mindset to figure it out.

I'll never have that problem again. Even if the housing market crashes or the stock market crashes, there are people who are not in that industry, who are in the health and fitness industry or the nutrition industry, who are doing well and are ready to level up. The specific industry doesn't even matter anymore.

ESTIMATE, THEN SHIFT

The biggest mistake I see others make when proving their own business model is: they quit. They think, "This isn't working. This one lead magnet isn't working (after a whole twelve people have seen it)." They shift too fast, are all over the place, and never become known for one thing. It's all about those one hundred days of intentional, focused work and being able to commit to becoming known for one thing and sticking with it no matter what. Truly listen to the marketplace and not just the pings of the marketplace. Quick hits don't tell you the full story.

> ## THE MAKEOVER METHOD™
> ## It's all about intentional, focused work and being able to commit to becoming known for one thing and sticking with it no matter what.
> MADEOVER

People ask, "But exactly where do I start? What if I start with a package or product that's priced way too high? Or too low?" Just like with math, if you can't get the exact answer, you estimate. To your best ability, estimate what you think your package and your message is going to be, and what it's worth in the marketplace. Consistently put it out there for a period of time until the feedback tells you how to shift. Then make small shifts at a time. If you make too many shifts, you can't tell which one is responsible for the positive change. Eventually, something will click, but you won't be sure what it was if you've implemented too many changes at one time.

Part of the process is discovering that, while you initially identify who you think your ideal client is, after you take action in the marketplace, it often turns out that you were a bit off base. It's the same principle as when you're niching down. You get to a point where you don't believe you can get any more specific. But there are always more layers. It's never-ending. That's why you have to fall in love with the process—being in the thick of the process never ends.

You might think your ideal client is a thirty-five-year-old female, but once you put your offering out into the marketplace, you might find that it's a forty-two-year-old male. Whether or not you switch your offer or your target demographic depends upon your core conviction. Using this example, if your mission in life is to help women, and upon releasing your offer you discover that the marketplace is telling you that your current offer is better geared toward men, you've got to tweak the offer. If your mission is only to prove your business model and sell some damn stuff and to whom you sell it isn't part of your core fundamental philosophy, then you need to shift your offer toward the demographic that's accepting it in the market.

I went through a period of time where I had an offer that was structured to appeal to new businesses. What I quickly learned was that most new businesses are broke and can't afford my services. I was going broke because I was going after a client who was broke. The whole thing wasn't working, and it was a complete mess by the time I recognized I needed to shift. My actual ideal client is an entrepreneur or business owner who's already successful but has a brand that's either amateur, ugly, confusing, or non-existent online.

One of my clients ran a $100 million roofing company but no online presence at all for his personal brand. Another helps brands build their Instagram presence and following, and he's doing great—he shows people how to travel the world for free—but he had no website. A third is a wildly successful NLP practitioner. His schedule is booked sixteen hours a day, but you'd never know it because he didn't ever get his website solidified. Half of it was still in *lorem ipsum*! On one hand, he doesn't care because his schedule's packed, but on the other hand he wants to help more people. He'll always have sixteen hours a day that can be dedicated to one-on-one clients, but he wants to be able to help thousands of people each month, and the only way for him to do that is to build an online portal that he can drive traffic to. In order to do that, his visual brand has to look the part. It's always about the moment when someone is ready to go to the next level and just hasn't had or taken the time to match their visual identity to where they are.

The shift happened when I stopped thinking I knew it all and began to truly listen to the marketplace, which was telling me that there are lots of people who actually have the money and the success to start putting themselves out there more. They recognize that if they put themselves out there as they are, people are going to view their website and be confused. Or try to find their website and not be able to because they don't have one. Once I started listening to the marketplace in that way, I had people happily paying me $9,900 to $49,900 for my products and services and waiting in line to do it.

My ideal client is willing to invest in their complete brand. Clients who are only prepared to spend a small amount tend to put too much emphasis on the logo, believing that the logo is what represents the totality of their visual brand. When business owners are at the point where spending $97 or $300 feels like a huge decision, they tend to want to feel a huge sense of control over the logo. It's not about the logo, it's about your entire business image.

THE MAKEOVER METHOD™

It's not about the logo, it's about your entire business image.

MADEOVER

START WITH A SIMPLE MVP

When I accepted investment capital several years ago to start the financial literacy company, my partner was my friend, Larry Jackson, Jr. ("Buggy") He'd been in Todd Ballenger's group with me, worked for Alpine, and wanted to leave the industry. I honestly didn't know what the fuck I was doing on several levels. I used investment capital to pay myself, which was completely stupid. I could have not taken the money, brought on a few people instead, paid them, not paid for massive website development, etc. There was just so much I didn't know, and that's part of the process any entrepreneur goes through. You can't look at those instances as failures or mistakes. They're opportunities to learn. Painful lessons, yes. But still opportunities.

If I could go back and do that all over again, I would first create a Minimum Viable Product and prove that our product was something people actually wanted and would buy. Money runs out quickly when you start hiring and paying other people while simultaneously not knowing what the hell you're doing! I could have properly proven the business model and not taken the investment capital. I could have had a nearly identical experience and not lost all the money. But this is how we learn.

Try to keep a high-level perspective when you're proving your business model. Not every single client is your ideal client, and so you have to be careful when issues arise that make you question whether the problem is with your business model or your client. We had a situation once where we weren't nailing it with a client's brand the way I'd hoped we would. Instead of getting completely down on myself, anxious, and jumping to reframe my business model, I identified where the confusion was coming from, how my team and I could add to the set of up-front expectations we provide to clients, and then fast-forwarded, realizing that the worst thing that could happen was that this client would never be fully satisfied. And that would be okay. I'd continue to build relationships and hone my communication process.

BE GRATEFUL FOR THE HICCUPS

I realized through this process that I'm so grateful for the hiccups because they force me to become better, to hone my process again and again. I knew once I had a 12-stage process documented with brand strategy, positioning, and showing my clients how to effectively run their own brand engine, that I was worth the premium fees we charge. Many of my clients start with us thinking they are going to get a killer new look, but they have no idea we are about to change their entire business and life with the value we provide through our experience.

Part of proving your business model is a continual honing of not only who your clients are but also how you handle chaos in terms of leading it to a solution versus declaring, "This isn't the right client for me." There's a fine line between the two approaches. It's about being able to take a look at yourself in the mirror and stop seeing things with emotion; you have to see things objectively. You have to ask yourself, "Is this client being crazy and picky and overly emotional?" The ability to do that is one of my superpowers. I have empathy, and I can put myself in someone else's shoes and retell the story from his perspective. With one such challenging moment, I was able to identify that my client had been successful for a couple of years, and his brand looked like shit. He looked like an amateur. He was all over the place, he knew it, and he'd already tried to solve the problem a couple of times without success. He's busy; that's why he hires people like me.

I made the decision to continue going through the process with him to see if I could turn it around. It was very frustrating for both of us in the beginning, but I also knew that the five referrals he sent to me are all wonderful! So, perhaps what I was faced with was a client who didn't know exactly what he needed. The question was, how could I help him? If he has clarity, does he go on his way and leave me with a bucket of referrals? I needed to feel comfortable that he trusted me, and we finally got there. There was just a difference in our personalities, the ways we approach life, and the ways we communicate. We're very different people, but that doesn't mean that either of us is inherently right or wrong. We had to figure out a way to communicate in a way that satisfied both of our needs.

THE MAKEOVER METHOD™

An increased confidence and not taking everything personally greatly helps you when you're navigating challenging situations.

MADEOVER

An increased confidence and willingness not to take everything personally greatly helps when you're navigating this sort of a situation. This client wasn't judging. He wasn't bagging on me or critiquing me. He was just asking, "Is there a better way to do this? How can you help me because I'm not happy with the way all this looks, and I haven't been for years." It didn't mean that he was never going to be happy. It didn't mean that he was saying, "Mike, you suck." Those inferences would all have been in my head were I to have had them (and there was definitely a time when I would have).

My approach was to go back and ask, "How can I make you happy?" It was that simple. His answer was equally simple: "I want to get the look I want, and I don't know what to do to get it. I don't understand the framework or how to write copy." Once I had complete clarity on his actual concerns, we dove into helping with those specific areas. He's a process driver, so he's used to deliverables being ready on his timeline. He once asked me for something that could easily take three or four weeks. An hour after asking me for it, he emailed me to see if it was finished yet. He was just excited and ready to share some of the new designs with his audience. My initial instinct was to tell him to go fuck himself. I mean, I almost started to type out a note and say, "Let's get something straight: I'm not your personal assistant, and you don't control my business." But I quickly recognized that wasn't going to be super effective. I'd just turned this relationship around for God's sake! So I chose not to respond.

I checked in with my designer on the status, and as soon as it was ready (which by some miracle ended up being just a few hours later), I sent it over to him and said, "They weren't finished when you pinged me earlier. I had two meetings, and just got out of the last one, but here they are." Just as I have, he's worked at his craft for a long time. While we don't deeply connect on a personal level, we've both tried a ton of shit in our businesses. We both built something from the ground up. He too wants to see others succeed. We go about things in very different ways, but we have that one common thread that we can return to.

The one attribute I want people to remember about me is that I'm always able to find the bright side of a situation. I'm able to ascertain what an experience is trying to teach me. In this case, I asked myself, "What could have been different about the experience in order not to have this client communicate that he was disappointed in my work?" When I looked back, I recognized that I didn't do a good enough job of explaining the full process to him. I didn't clarify what was going to happen first, second, and third. I didn't proactively direct the conversation in that direction. I didn't set boundaries. I didn't say, "This is what I'm *not* going to do for you as part of this package." At the end of the day, it was a communication issue. I didn't communicate well enough what the process was going to be, and he was disappointed because he didn't yet have clarity with his brand strategy. Brand strategy wasn't one of the services I was providing, so I communicated that he was going to need to get clarity on his copy before I could effectively help. That was the disconnect. This experience compelled me to create a $25,000 package that was already going to be created, but it forced me to get clear on it sooner than later and start documenting every single stage of my process and build a system around the process as a whole. I broke my process into twelve stages, added a money-back guarantee, and documented every step of our process, which I hadn't done before. I now know that on Day 9, such-and-such happens. Everything is documented, has a checklist, and is systematized so things get done without fail, every time.

Earlier in my career, when these kinds of "bad" things happened, it often set me way back. I didn't identify a solution-focused response; I had more of a "This isn't working; this isn't going to work" mentality. A lot of that was rooted in my self-confidence issues. Any remark could really hurt my already-low confidence. At one point, Clay asked me, "When can a comment just be a comment instead of a personal attack on you? It's just a comment."

I now know that I don't have all the answers. There is no perfect approach. We're all flowing with life the best we can, and I really do try and keep an open mind at every opportunity. Even when I had a disappointed client, I asked, "What's this trying to teach me?" instead of saying, "Fuck this guy. He can go fuck himself." I recognize that my frustration stems from the fact that my system is not yet fully in place, or I'm not taking control of the project in the way that I should.

LAUNCH AND TWEAK

You prove your business model only up until the point where you launch because you have to have the real-world experiences in order to allow you to pivot, add, delete, or modify. You cannot prove your business model in a vacuum.

THE MAKEOVER METHOD™

You cannot prove your business model in a vacuum.

MADEOVER

Your business model is always evolving, and you will be honing it forever. I'm still proving my business model because I'm not satisfied with staying stagnant. The question is always, "How can I make it better?" and I identify what I can tweak to improve it.

It's a continual narrowing of focus that you get only through action and experience. That realization has given me a lot of peace—just having that internal knowing that I'm never going to be at a point where I say, "This is 100% the thing, and it's fixed." The truth will always be, this is the thing *for now*. There will always be an *aha* moment or a lightbulb that goes on, and that's what I enjoy. I enjoy the growth process, personally and professionally. It's about learning to embrace it and seeing the obstacles as challenges to run toward. Every obstacle is an experience that's showing me something that can be improved.

When you're working with clients at your highest price points, those clients are going to be more particular. You therefore have to evolve your knowledge and your skills in order to communicate better with that type of person instead of saying, "Piss Off." Not only have my instincts gotten better but I've also improved my reactions when things don't go as planned. It bothers me very little anymore when things go off-course. When a relationship isn't a good fit, I don't view it as wasted time anymore. I view it as time I invested in learning something about myself—a better way to sell, a better way to explain my process, a better way to structure my package.

After recognizing that I needed to be clearer about the structure of my process, especially with our higher-end clients, I put together an email within which I laid out my method and my process for all of my prospects. Once a client invests, I have a landing page that provides the client with all the interview questions we need them to answer. Once that's complete, they're sent to another landing page to tackle the next step. With this system in place, I can efficiently manage so many more clients because the process is systematized. I know that, for example, we're on Week 2 with such-and-such client, and therefore, this is what's going on this week. It was painfully slow to get all that content created because it took me forever to get it out of my head and documented.

Our process is so dialed at this point that it won't shift terribly much in the future. We have twelve stages to makeover a brand, and the entire process takes approximately twelve weeks. I'm very clear on what happens each and every week (three months to change our clients' businesses and lives forever—not bad!). I created an anchor with my high-ticket product, which makes my lower-end offers more palatable. I created a three-payment option. Because the process takes three months, we might as well give clients a three-month payment option. We also tell clients they can cancel for any reason in the first thirty days. That risk-reversal feature over the first thirty days was well received. They can fire us; we can fire them—for any reason. It gives us both the chance to get to day twenty-nine and say, "I don't like working with you." In most cases, the clients are ecstatic to continue after those first those days because so much value has been provided already.

Once you have proven your business model in the marketplace, you can move on to the next phase, The Makeover Strategy™.

You can find all of The Makeover Method™ resources on our website:

https://themakeovermaster.com/resources

THE MAKEOVER STRATEGY™

*Developing a strategy to consistently
articulate who you are and what you
represent will grow your following, your
business and give you peace of mind.*

O nce you've proven your business model, it's time
to figure out your brand strategy. When it comes
to creating your brand strategy, soliciting an
objective outside perspective is critical. Regardless of all
my years of study, one thing I can't give myself is outside
perspective in order to gain necessary clarity. Don't try to
do this part on your own because it's not possible to give
yourself your own outside perspective.

The fastest way to learn anything is to decide what you
want, find somebody who already knows the answer, and
hire that person to help you get there faster. If you're going
to try to do it alone, there are efficient and inefficient levels
of that approach. I could pay somebody $5,000 to coach
me for four weeks, or I could pay them $100 and read all
their materials and go through their online course(s) in
order to attempt it on my own. The former, if at all
feasible, is far more productive over the short term. The

worst thing you can do is invest in something—whether it's a $20 or a $2,000 investment—without being completely clear about why you're investing in it. If you don't have that clarity, that money could go elsewhere.

THE MAKEOVER METHOD™

Brand strategy boils down to one word: clarity.

MADEOVER

Brand strategy boils down to one word: clarity. Potential customers don't take action when they're not clear on exactly what you have to offer. When I was growing up, my dad used to say, "Remember who you are and what you represent" whenever I went to a party or a function of some sort. It stuck with me because he said it so often. Brand strategy comes down to having clarity on who you are, what you represent, and how you want to be perceived in the marketplace. Last—but definitely not least—what action or actions are you going to take in the next day or week so that more people find out who you are and what you represent?

OUTSIDE PERSPECTIVE
AND CLARITY AROUND MY BRAND

I'll never forget Desislava Dobreva sitting down with me in Thailand at the Opposed Media compound and working through my brand strategy from her perspective. Desi has a master's degree in branding and really knows her stuff. Her help was a huge turning point for me with my brand.

It was the first time I began to see how powerful I actually was, and believe it. She listed out my backstory and my purpose, and talked through all the stuff I'd been through. As I saw myself and my brand on paper, the way I could communicate and help others all began to make sense. We met one other time to talk through my brand strategy about thirty days later. I'll always be grateful for her advice and perspective because the truth is, I never would have seen my own strengths without having someone looking in from the outside.

A few months later, as I continued to tighten up my message and brand strategy, I met Fanny Myth, a brand strategist from France. It was time for me to take my brand a level deeper. I could be clearer, and I needed that outside perspective again. Honestly, I had taken so much action during those first few months after the Project Persuasion event that I had evolved to the point where I again became a bit confused.

Fanny and I worked together for four weeks through her coaching process, and my message really came together. I knew who I was as a brand, what I stood for.

and how I was going to communicate that to the marketplace.

Today, I have my brand strategy, my own philosophies around branding, and my brand engine in total alignment. I work with clients and speak to groups on how they can clarify their brands and take action to get the businesses and lives they want. But, were it not for these two wonderful ladies and their outside perspectives, my brand wouldn't have developed so quickly.

My point is, don't try to figure it all out on your own. Outside perspective is critical, and something you'll never be able to give yourself.

CREATING YOUR AUTHENTIC MOVIE ROLE

The clients we work with through our Brand Makeover Experience™ discover what I call your "authentic movie role," and how they can put it all together.

As you begin working on your brand for the first time, it can feel overwhelming when it comes to how to do it all and even where to begin. I was always wanting someone to just tell me what to do. I wanted them to peel back the curtain and show me how to run my day-to-day operations. Creating your authentic movie role is the first step in that process.

I've heard stories of A-list actors who go into a role and never break character. It's called method acting, and some of the very best do it. In preparation for *The Revenant*, Leonardo DiCaprio reportedly camped outside for eight weeks. He also slept inside an animal carcass and ate a raw bison. When Jim Carrey was filming *The Man on the Moon*,

I've heard that people started thinking he was crazy because he was always acting like Andy Kaufman and insisted on being called Andy at all times, even between scenes. They stay in character throughout the filming of the movie. Never. Breaking. Character. Ever.

THE MAKEOVER METHOD™

Never break character. Ever.

MADEOVER

That's brand strategy—knowing your movie role and how you're going to play it inside and out. If you have a strong brand, you never break character. Even in private. That's an area where it took me a bit longer to re-train my brain. I remember a time early on, sitting with Mac on the back deck of the Opposed Media compound in Thailand, saying, "Fuck. I have $236 in my checking account." He responded, "Nobody needs to know that, dude." Literally, no one needs to know that (besides my wife!). Many of us have one person with whom we share everything, and we can break character with them, but that's it.

That's how you need to think about your brand. You don't hide behind your position, you *become* your position, as my good friend and mentor Mitch Miller once said to me. To do this, you need to be very clear on what your brand actually is, what you stand for and, equally as important, what you stand *against*.

It's not just your movie role, and it isn't about faking anything. Your brand is authentic and genuine, and documenting it on paper will give you clarity like you've never had before. Once you do this, a tremendous weight is lifted from your shoulders because you can now stay in character 24/7/365. This is what it's all about—having such clarity around who you are, why you do what you do, what you stand for, and what you stand against. Plus, you understand your journey, how you became the man or woman you are today. Get this part right, and you'll see a consistency in your brand like you've never before experienced.

In the next few sections, I'll work backward through your brand strategy to help you build it from the ground up. You have to start with a solid foundation, your core driving force.

CORE DRIVING FORCE

In 2006, I was less than two months into my marriage when I came home from work, and Katie said, "We need to talk." I remember thinking, "Oh crap, what did I do this time?" when the following words came out of her mouth:

"I'm pregnant."

I was shocked, but only because we hadn't even thought about kids. We hadn't even taken our honeymoon yet, and it wasn't in our short-term plans. We talked a lot that night, and we agreed that someday, we were going to go down this road and create a family, so now was as good a time as any. Hell, I've always just jumped into to everything else; why should this be any different?

On March 2, 2007, I became a father to my son, Jeffrey. I call the day your first child is born "the day the world disappears." There is no work, no emails, no phone calls, no meetings, no anything that matters more or can distract you from being present in that moment. It's a wonderful feeling and day. It's also the day when you realize a love that you've never had before, the love for a child.

Almost two years later to the day, we had our daughter, Lucy. With my family complete, I knew I would do anything for them. I had a new mission in life: not to give my kids everything so they didn't have to struggle but instead to become a role model to them and show them how to develop their own path, their own journey. I knew that kids model their parents' behavior, and my goal was to make damn sure they didn't make some of the mistakes I'd already made.

At some point back when I was starting out as an entrepreneur in 2008, I made a decision and created a mindset around what this all meant. I developed a deep inner purpose, my core driving force in life. The story I told myself early on was that my kids were going to model the behavior of their mom and dad. I was already on the path going after my ideal lifestyle, my dreams. So if I quit, if I gave up on that journey, it would show my kids exactly how to settle in life. How to give up on your dreams and go get a job in a cubicle, a bank job, a 401k, and a cheap gold watch. They'd watch a man live a life of misery because he quit on his dreams too early. They would think that their dreams weren't possible, and they wouldn't go after them. That's how they'd model my behavior.

Fuck that.

When people hear my entire story and the decade-long journey filled with two periods of going "broke," they often ask me why I didn't quit, give up, and get a 9-5 job to pay the bills. My answer to clients and others I coach through The Makeover Method™ is, pick a core driving force, one that the thought of is more painful than the pain of quitting. If you do that, as I have, you will never quit. No obstacle, no misstep, no mistake, would ever be worth quitting to me. In my mind, showing my kids that it's okay to live a settled life and not go after your dreams is more painful than quitting.

> ### THE MAKEOVER METHOD™
>
> ## Pick a core driving force, one that the thought of is more painful than the pain of quitting.
>
> MADEOVER

When you keep that core driving force in your mind, you'll make it through all adversity. I can't state how important this step is as you develop your brand strategy. It's mandatory.

BUSINESS DRIVING FORCE

The next step is a secondary purpose that I call the business driving force. It's what will help you get out of bed every morning and keep you energized about your work. I've gone through a lot of my story already, so I'll spare you from repeating it. But my business driving force is a result of my personal journey and all the years I struggled to figure this stuff out for myself.

It's simple.

Who will I meet today who is struggling by putting myself out there? Maybe they haven't struggled for a decade. Maybe it's only been six months or a year, maybe two years. But their struggle is real, just as mine was. Their pain is real, and they need someone's help, someone who can relate and show them the path to break free. They need a friend, a mentor, a coach, and a guide who will be there for them.

This is why I get up every morning and do what I do. It's not about the money. It's not about the logo, social media, and website appearance. It's about the makeover, the transformation of a life and the lives of those my clients can impact.

Someone like my friend Clay Moffat, known as the B.A.D. entrepreneur and my mindset wizard (aka coach). When we met, his brand was amateur at best in terms of the way it appeared online. This guy was literally changing people and saving lives with his services, helping people with PTSD and suicidal thoughts as well as entrepreneurs suffering from major burn out, anxiety, and depression. But how many more lives could he save and change if his brand looked the part and showcased who he truly is? He was leaving impact and money on the table by not getting his image in order, and we worked through our makeover experience together and fixed his business image so he could have more influence, power, and respect, and help more people with his wizardry.

That's why I get up every day. Who is going to be the next brand to change the world if I help them get their brand and business image in order?

You need to know your business driving force so that you have the energy to get up and get to work any and every day you choose.

MILESTONE STORIES

We all have stories, and they can change the world if you document them and can articulate them to others. Milestone stories are part of the journey that has led you to the person you are today. Understanding the three to five major life events that had the most impact on you is important. It's through these milestone stories that you are going to attract your following, the people who resonate and connect with you as a person. They need to know that you are not perfect. They need to know you and your struggles and what you've made it through to get to where you are today.   My milestone stories are…

• My unfulfilled journey to become a professional baseball player

• My decade-long journey in the mortgage industry and growing a company from scratch

• My first entrepreneurial failure

• My success as the Number Two in command behind the scenes

• The $200,000 struggle and second period of going broke

THE MAKEOVER METHOD™

Your stories have power.

MADEOVER

Your stories have power and should make you realize that you have also been through adversity and overcome it. Recognize and document your three to five stories, and share them with the world so you can attract others who want to connect with you, learn from you, and ultimately, pay you and work with you.

YOUR ANIMAL, CHARACTER, VALUES, MINDSET AND PERSONALITY

This section of your brand strategy is taking all of the important stuff and breaking it down into a synopsis, a Cliff's Notes version of who you are today.

I was working with my speaking coach, Ariane de Melo, aka "The Branding Director" when she taught me a technique called Creating Your Spirit Animal. It's used in acting to help you quickly get into character. For the record, my animal is an old wise bear with scars on his face and body from the battles he's survived. He sits by the river watching his mate and cubs play in the river while he enjoys protecting them and watching them enjoy the sunny day. He occasionally jumps into the river with them, digging out a fish and handing it to them. When he's done, he slowly strolls over to the trees, scratches his back, and takes a rest.

This is an overview of my brand, my character, and I think of this old battle-survived bear before I speak on stage, before I go into client meetings, before I hop on a Facebook Live or sales call, and it immediately puts me into the right frame of mind. I've also created a short paragraph on my character and documented my values, mindset, and personality traits. All of this clarity in my brand strategy gives me the confidence and consistency to be on brand, 24/7/365.

As I said before, this isn't about faking anything. It's documenting who you are and what you represent at a level most people haven't explored. It's why so many are confused as to why their business isn't working, and there's a negative number in their bank account.

You can see my brand strategy deep dive document in the resources section on our website. It can also be found at https://themakeovermaster.com/deepdive

THE BUSINESS SHORT

Honestly, if you ever meet me in person, I can be a bit awkward. I'm still quite the introvert, and my days of true self-confidence issues linger in public situations like parties.

If you approach me, I sometimes struggle with the question, "So, what do you do?"

This is why I needed a business short. I had to be able to articulate who I am and what I do quickly and in a way that people could easily understand.

I work with entrepreneurs who have a personal brand that is amateur, ugly, confusing, or non-existent. It's costing them money, influence, power, and respect in their niche. We provide a brand makeover experience so they can look the part of who they truly are and know what to do next to increase their income and impact. Our clients are able to change more lives and make more money after working with us.

You, too, need to develop a business short that is easy to express and that articulates who you help and how you help them.

TAGLINE AND SUB-TAGLINE

When I'm introduced by others these days, people say, "I'd like you to meet Mike Young; he's known as The Makeover Master." I'll admit, saying I'm the master of anything still feels a bit arrogant and awkward to me. But I needed to create a title by which people could remember me and and easily repeat to others.

Mike Young, The Makeover Master.

Your business image is costing you money, influence, power, and respect. You are finally successful, it's time to start looking like it.

It's an easy way for me to articulate what I do, and people can repeat that tagline and sub-tagline and remember me for the impact I provide.

STAY IN YOUR LANE AND CONSISTENT COMMUNICATION

Solidifying your brand strategy requires that you know your brand values, your character, your stories, and your personal and business purpose. Once you have this all down, it's time to move on to the next phase of The Makeover Method™, The Makeover Image: It's time you look the part of who you truly are.

You can find all of The Makeover Method™ resources on our website:

https://themakeovermaster.com/resources

THE MAKEOVER IMAGE™

Like it or not, people do still judge books based on their covers.

Think of your brand strategy as your internal strategy with regard to the character you're going to play in your authentic movie role. Your business image (aka your visual brand identity) is all about a client's first impression. It's all about the way your clients perceive you. Honestly, so many successful people have done very well without getting this part right. I'm friends with plenty of business killers in every industry that have built seven, eight, and even nine-figure businesses who don't look the part. Their visual brand identity doesn't reflect who they truly are and the impact they are having. And it's costing them money, influence, power, and respect in their niche. Sure, you can be successful without a solid visual brand identity, but consider how much more you could do and how many more people you could help if you got your business image in order? How many more people would engage with you and your business for the very first time if you didn't look amateur, ugly, confusing, or non-existent?

THE MAKEOVER METHOD™

Your visual brand identity could be costing you money, influence, power and respect in your niche.

MADEOVER

Your business image is defined as Everything a new prospect can see with their eyes to form a first impression of you and your business to determine whether or not they choose to contact you and take the first step.

Everything.

Your business image is so much more than fancy logos, fonts, and colors. It's made up of everything people can see to form an impression of you and decide whether it's worth it to contact you. It's made up of (but not limited to) the following components:

- Your Logo
- Professional, High-Quality Images
- Mobile Responsiveness
- Consistency
- Typography
- Color Palette
- Alignment, Spacing & Sizing

- Social Media Posting Consistency
- Proof
- Social Proof
- Online Interactions & Comments
- Pricing
- Availability
- Reviews
- Search Engine Results
- Gossip & Buzz
- High & Low Status Behaviors
- Link Flow & Broken Links
- And More…

Think of it this way: If you ran across yourself for the very first time online and decided to spend two full hours engaging in a Google search and clicking every link on your website, every review, essentially stalking yourself across all social media, what would you think? Are you amateur, ugly, confusing, and/or non-existent? Or are you professional, pretty, clear, and present? Would you contact and buy from you? Would you find a hundred posts about your cat and negative comments on social media that scared you away?

All of this collectively makes up your business image, and when it's not right, people run away from you. And typically, they never come back.

To break it down into approaches you can take to fix your image, there are four main concepts from neuroscience (how our brains work) that you need to understand. An understanding of these concepts will solve your business image and the way you think about it forever. The four concepts are:

- First Impressions
- Cognitive Bias
- Cognitive Fluency
- Neuroendocrine Reactivity

If you have proven your business model and developed a strategy to deploy your message, it's time to dress up your brand so that it looks the part.

FIRST IMPRESSIONS

I remember the day I met my wife. It was Saturday, June 30, 2001, and we met walking up to the Hillsboro airshow of all places. I'd never been to an airshow, and I've not been back since. But somehow, on this day, we met.

We both had friends who worked at a bar in Portland, and they were hosting a tent at the airshow filled with free food and a lot of alcohol. I was walking up to the tent with my best friend at the time, Terry. It was a hot day, and we had already had a beer or two when I saw her.

She was this cute, tiny little thing in jean shorts, a white tank top, a small tattoo on the back of her neck, and pigtails. She had an amazing smile and laugh, and I'm not going to lie, she was hot. I knew I wanted to get to know her more.

I did get a chance to introduce myself and talk with her for a bit that day, and I really liked her personality, sense of humor, and zest for life. I left hoping I'd get to see her again and get to know more about her. I later found out that a few hours after we met, she had drunk too much and got really sick, throwing up right next to where my car was parked only hours before.

I've often wondered what would have happened if we had met while she was throwing up? Would we have ended up together? I can honestly say I don't think so; the first impression she made was outstanding, and if our timing had been different that day, I joke that it probably would have cost me my wife, kids, and everything I have today.

In business, the first impression you make matters when it comes to attracting clients who want to get to know you more and take that first step with your brand.

Are you looking great, or are you throwing up in the parking lot?

First impressions are formed by the brain in about one-tenth of a second, and unless you are blind, it's first formed with what we see. I see so many businesses focused on their sales conversion rates. When people do get to a sales conversation, what is the percentage of people who actually buy? These businesses spend a lot of time trying to improve their conversion rate, but the truth is, that number is based on a variety of factors such as lead quality, sales skills, proof, social proof, and the strength of the offer. And it typically doesn't change much without a lot of work over months or years.

There is a much easier way to grow your business faster without messing around for years on your sales conversion rate.

First, double the number of people who see you for the very first time.

Second, get your entire business image dialed in and on point.

If you do those two things, your opportunities and number of sales conversations will go through the roof. You can even still suck at sales and only convert ten to twenty-five percent of those people. But, if you are talking with one hundred people instead of three, your business will grow. It all starts with giving yourself a chance and creating a great first impression.

COGNITIVE BIAS

When I was growing up, I bought into the "American Dream." I held onto that belief for almost thirty years. And then I had all of that. I'd accomplished the dream, and I was miserable. It required that arrive at and experience that place in reality to have the wisdom to know what it felt like to be in debt up to my eyeballs, working eighteen-hour days to keep it going. I'm not saying that you can't have a lot of money and nice things. What I'm saying, in fact, is that you can have all that stuff *and not be miserable*. I just got ahead of myself and did it in the way that far too many others do as well, through mortgages and bank loans.

Why did I hold onto this belief for almost thirty years? Because of cognitive bias.

Cognitive bias is what our brains are designed to do. We hold onto a presented belief system until it's dramatically proven otherwise. It's the reason why murder mysteries and thriller movies work so well. They present us with an idea early in the movie, and we hold onto that idea until they twist it on us toward the end. Just like every episode of *Scooby Doo* ever created. "Holy cow, it was old man Smithers after all!"

This is why your first impression matters so damn much. People will judge you quickly and then hold onto that original belief until they are proven otherwise over time. Honestly, most bad first impressions never get a chance to recover. Prospects see your confusing business image and move on to another business that seems to have their act together and a solution to their problem. When that first impression is out of alignment with the way you want your brand to be perceived, there's an issue.

A great example of this phenomenon in action was my friend and co-author, Elizabeth Lyons. She helps entrepreneurs write, publish, and launch their books, and is known (now) as "The Entrepreneurs' Author." While that was her area of expertise, before she hired us to makeover her brand, my first impression of her based on her website at the time was more about jewelry and apparel (and books). She wasn't presenting herself as the high-performing entrepreneurs' author and book coach she's become known for being. She was confusing as all hell to new prospects, and it was costing her money. Since working with us, her average sale has increased by over 1200%, and she is at full capacity with a waiting list.

COGNITIVE FLUENCY

Our brains are lazy bastards.

This is why you see so many articles titled "The 3 simple steps to save money" and "5 quick hacks to regain your health."

We want to be told what to do in the simplest and fastest way possible, and we don't want to waste time trying to figure it out on our own. Hell, even the side of a Pop Tarts box includes "The 3 Steps to Heat Up Your Pop Tart." Step 1: Remove from the package. (Duh) Step 2: Put in microwave. Step 3: Heat 30 seconds and enjoy. You wouldn't think we would need such simple instructions, but the truth is, humans prefer to be told what to do. If your site doesn't present them with *one* simple place to start, you are costing yourself money and new customers.

There is a book titled *Intimate Behavior* by Desmond Morris wherein he discusses the natural progression humans go through from first meeting to having intercourse. People who don't know you or your business go through a similar journey, a relationship with you, before they buy. You can go through these stages very quickly, but you can't skip more than two at a time or it doesn't work.

Just so you know, the twelve stages are:
- Eye to Body
- Eye to Eye
- Voice to Voice
- Hand to Hand (or Arm)
- Arm to Shoulder
- Arm to Waist (or Back)
- Mouth to Mouth
- Hand to Head
- Hand to Body
- Mouth to Breast
- Hand to Genitals
- Genitals to Genitals

My point is, if you don't tell people exactly where to begin a relationship with you, they won't. Stop confusing the shit out of people and trying to sleep with them (sell them something) on your first date. It rarely works. Tell them where to begin, and allow the relationship to develop into a sale.

NEUROENDOCRINE REACTIVITY

This can be described as your "sixth sense." It's that feeling you get in your body when something feels right or wrong, without knowing for sure or being able to describe it.

It reminds me of the time I took my family with me on a business trip to Puerto Rico to attend Mitch Miller's and and Bobby Stocks' Total Facebook Domination event. I was there to meet entrepreneurs and share my story from the stage.

We'd never been there before.

Just like when you visit any new place for the first time, we didn't know where to go on the first night there. We didn't know which restaurants were good, and which were crap. The first night, we went out as a family and decided to wing it and try a restaurant without doing much research. We were walking around Old San Juan, a beautiful and colorful city, when a waiter came up to us on the street and said we should come inside for the best mofongo in Puerto Rico. Something felt off, but we were hungry and decided to go inside to eat. The waitress took several minutes to come over before handing us a menu and taking our drink order. That should have been my cue that this was not going to be a great experience, but I'm a patient guy, and we were hungry, I didn't want to look for another place.

It never got better. Our meal arrived almost an hour later and was less than stellar. The whole experience went down as my gut could have predicted just two hours earlier on the street with the waiter. It was my sixth sense, my gut, my intuition, call it whatever you want, I knew it was going to suck from the start, and I should have listened to my gut.

That's neuroendocrine reactivity. It's the sense you get right off the bat. It can't be described, but we all have it and know the feeling.

This is going to be good.

This is going to suck.

Many times, we know before we even begin that movie, that dinner, or that trip whether it's going to be great or be a bust. Your prospects' sixth sense results from your business image. Everything they see with their eyes to form a first impression of you, and their choice as to whether or not to contact you and give you a chance to earn their business determines whether they feel good about you or you're not for them.

A part of neuroendocrine reactivity is a concept known as "cognitive dissonance." It's what makes our bodies and minds have trouble and react negatively when presented with conflicting ideas simultaneously.

This is why I spend so much time with clients throughout our 12-stage makeover experience to get their business image in order, to do it right. It's literally the life and death of your business. Get it right, and you'll have a waiting list and premium prices. Get it wrong, and you'll be chasing customers and scraping by, competing on price.

Yes, your business image has a bit to do with fonts and colors and logos, but the real lynchpin is the overall perception and first impression of your brand. People look at your brand and make a decision on who you who you are before they even read the copy. Your image matters, and when you don't get it right, the negative consequences are undeniable.

You can find all of The Makeover Method™ resources on our website:

https://themakeovermaster.com/resources

THE MAKEOVER
INFLUENCE™

The influence you display online is directly tied to the speed of client acquisition, your business growth and impact you will have with your brand.

When I attended Project Persuasion in Phuket, I met Ulyses Osuna. Ulyses is the CEO of Influencer Press and the creator of the Manufacturing Influence concept.

He was a 20-year-old kid but had the business and speaking persona of a seasoned veteran. I remember him communicating that the term "manufactured influence" could be perceived as faking your influence when, in fact, manufacturing your influence has nothing to do with faking anything. It's about choosing to display what you want your prospects and audience to see, and removing posts and content that you *don't* necessarily want them to see or that might confuse them. Manufacturing your influence is really about displaying the truth of who you already are in an organized, public way. It's not about manufacturing your story. It's about intentionally showcasing the story of who you already are. And it's a big part of your overall business image.

Once you have proven your business model, your strategy is in place, and you look the part, the next phase of The Makeover Method™ is about reach and growth. It's time to put some real fuel to your fire and get your name out there. You need to go from being seen by hundreds per day to thousands, or from thousands to tens of thousands. It's time to increase the number of people seeing you for the first time and grow your following.

THE MAKEOVER METHOD™

Growing your influence in your niche is a process of being clear about what you want your audience to see.

MADEOVER

Growing your influence in your niche is a process of being clear about what you want your audience to see. It's not lying in any way; it's not saying you were featured in *Forbes* if you were not. It's having intentional control over what people see to ensure that they see all the good things.

There are a ton of ways to show influence, and I won't go into every single one in this chapter. What I will say is that it can be broken down into understanding what "growing your influence" actually means in the simplest of terms.

PROOF

This is where you show proof that you are an authority in your space, and there are a few areas I focus on with my business. It may simplify things for you to follow my lead.

- Public Speaking
- Facebook Lives
- Podcasts
- TV Shows
- Publications
- Proof of Results

So many people in the world are deathly afraid of speaking in public or putting themselves out there in any way. You can shortcut your authority simply by putting yourself out there consistently. Most people don't.

When it comes to new prospects engaging with you and buying from you, understand that proof of results, social proof, reviews, and testimonials are huge.

I'll show you exactly where I focus in the next chapter, but for now I'll share that my primary focus when it comes to manufacturing my influence is consistent documentation of our makeovers—both the acquisition of new clients and their new brand launches. After that, consistently speaking in public, both on stage and on

Facebook, podcasts, and TV shows. Finally, getting articles and publications written about myself, my story, and my philosophies when it comes to branding and business image.

When I became "The Makeover Master" and our model, strategy, and image were solid, I was still being mentored and coached by Mitch Miller and Macually Ryan with Opposed Media Company. Mitch told me it was time to blow up my reach, and I needed to become a "podcast whore." A lot more people needed to find out about me, and I could expedite that through podcasts, live speaking, publications, TV shows, Facebook Live events, and more. It was time for me to manufacture my influence.

I did two things, and I want to share them with you because I think far too many people forget the tools they have at their disposal. So many people say things like, "I would, if only I had the money" or "I wish I could, but I'm broke." I know this because I told myself these same lies for years and forgot that there are other ways to create an equal exchange of value, like bartering. People have done it since the earliest days of man, exchanging one thing of value for another. My coat for some food, or some gold for dental work. I hadn't yet built my empire to afford to do everything at once, and I needed to do the same thing: get creative.

I asked Ulyses Osuna if I could trade a brand makeover for him or anyone on his team in exchange for his PR services and help. I also found Nathan Ortega with Influencer Podcasts who was in need of his own brand makeover. They both said Yes, and our package prices were almost equivalent, so it made it an easy win/win.

There's nothing wrong with bartering in that way at any point in the growth of your business. A creative exchange of value is an approach that smart entrepreneurs have been utilizing for quite some time, and it was one of the most effective strategies I learned as I built my business. I will still consider bartering if it's the perfect relationship and the right deal, although I rarely do it anymore.

The simplest way to get started with the process of manufacturing your influence is to Google yourself and your business. Look at the Google results as well as the contents of all of your social media accounts—anything a new prospect would look at—and mentally put yourself into their shoes when you do it. What do you think? What's your first impression? Does this person seem to have their act together? Do they seem to know what they're doing?

People often don't employ strategic leverage in their business. As an example, you likely often get on a call with a new prospect and talk about who you are, what you represent, what you care about, and how your products and services work. And then you do it again the next day with someone new. And the next day. And the next day. Once you've properly manufactured your influence, you'll have so much press and publicity telling the same story you're telling people one by one, but it's leveraged in a far more efficient way.

People will quickly perceive your value based on what they can readily see, touch, and read. I had to spend months consistently posting on social media before I felt ready for a significant PR push. Once you're ready to take this next step, it's extremely helpful to find someone to help you. You can do it on your own to a degree, but once you're at a certain place in your business, doing so doesn't make sense. Why try to figure out four or five years' worth of PR lessons that someone else has already figured out? They've made all the mistakes for you, and therefore, make the process so much easier by emailing me and saying, "Here's a show you can be on. Here's their schedule. Pick a date." I then show up and do the podcast or Facebook Live interview or TV interview. That's what makes a solid PR firm worth it.

If you decide to hire someone to help you with this part of your branding, you need to be careful, however. There are so many people out there who are great with spin—not just on your story but on theirs. Use referrals and relationships to seek out a great fit. It's critical to work with someone who knows what he or she is doing when it comes to positioning you because publications can help your positioning or *hurt* your positioning, depending on who you are and where you are in the business-building and position-building process.

Ulyses Osuna with Influencer Press and Nathan Ortega with Influencer Podcasts are my current PR firm and podcast firm. They are great because they think through and about the media opportunities I'm positioned for as stepping stones of leverage. They know the process, and if they got me in a certain publication or on a show or podcast, it's a step to the next level. It enables me to get booked on higher-level shows or podcasts the next time. It's that kind of stepping-stone leverage that is efficient and effective.

The key to building your influence is making sure you document each publication, podcast, and TV appearance you are on. I'll talk about this more in the next chapter when I show you The Makeover Engine™.

I remember flying home from my first TV appearance on *Good Morning LA* with Dr. Erin Fall Haskell, Jezlan Moyet, and Robert Mack. I wanted to shout from the rooftops how excited I was for myself, my business, and my brand. But there is a fine line between displaying proof and hurting your status and positioning online by looking too excited.

Just keep putting yourself out there, sharing your experiences, and documenting the journey to your audience. Let the proof and influence speak for itself. There is a difference between a post that says, "OMG I WAS JUST ON GOOD MORNING LA! I CAN'T BELIEVE IT!" and one that says, "It was a lot of fun to share my story today on *Good Morning LA,* and the hosts couldn't have been more awesome to work with." The first post makes it look like I'm shocked to have been on TV; the latter makes it look as though I'm grateful, and it happens all the time.

THE MAKEOVER METHOD™

Have your content strategy figured out before going full bore on your PR and influence.

MADEOVER

When it comes to your influence, I highly recommend that you have your content strategy figured out before going full bore on your PR. After all, there's no point to manufacturing your influence if you're only going to tear it to shreds with one poorly thought-out social media post. I can think of so many examples of times brands have hurt their positioning in online groups. Groups, such as those on Facebook, are great because they make people feel like they're part of a community. However, all of a sudden people start using the group to help them solve challenges they should be solving privately. That's why it's so important to have a behind-the-scenes mastermind or network or support group—whatever you want to call it. I have a group of people I can bounce ideas off of privately. Or, here's a weird concept: use Google to get answers!

I saw a post a while ago where a girl said, "Hey guys! I'm having a really hard day. My relationship's not going well and blah blah blah…" I thought, "What the fuck are you doing? You're in a group with 22,000 people, and you're telling people them that you've got fundamental issues. Nobody's ever going to buy from you!" I see posts all the time where people ask, "How do I use Zoom?" or "How do I use Excel?" They're literally asking questions that can be answered by Google. I see people posting things like, "I'm trying to figure this out for my business and my ideal client," which literally confirms that they don't know their ideal client. But the next moment, they're trying to sell their products and services, even though they've just made it clear that they're still trying to figure out what those products and services are and who they're trying to sell them to!

I see people who clearly don't have their shit together—and, to be fair, none of us has all of our shit together; we're all in our own heads struggling with something—but there is a way to structure your life where you don't need to publicly display some of that stuff and still get the help you need. I can get all the help I need from four or five people instead of posting in a group of 45,000 and destroying not only my brand positioning but also my status. We all have issues, but don't publicly post about them. Don't post about your current self-confidence or limiting belief issues. When people do this, they don't recognize that they are showing that they have neither proven their business model nor developed a clear brand strategy.

The bottom line: people don't buy from broke or broken people. Remember that as you put yourself out there online.

All of that is work you can and should figure out on your own or with your inner circle. Even though I coach against it now, I used to make this mistake all the time. I'd build my first landing page and then post it in a huge group and ask, "What do you guys think of this?" And then I wondered why people weren't buying from me.

Now it's time to put all this knowledge into your brand engine and be deadly consistent.

You can find all of The Makeover Method™ resources on our website:

https://themakeovermaster.com/resources

THE MAKEOVER ENGINE™

***You get to decide where to steer the car and
how much to apply the gas or the brakes, but
your engine should always be running and
well maintained.***

A t 4:31 one morning recently, my alarm went off, and my body evidently decided to ignore that. I woke up at 7:15 instead. That was when the failure story began. "I didn't do my morning glory meditation, cube meditation, journaling, or learning. I somehow managed to sleep right through all of it. The day is wrecked."

That's what I initially told myself. But I then realized that the story I'd told myself was a huge lie. In fact, it was 7:15am, and the world was my oyster. I had an entire day still ahead of me. I reframed my thoughts. I reminded myself to breathe, ask myself what the truth really is, ask myself what I could still control, and get back on track.

I took my kids to school and had a great hot yoga session with my wife. I then had an interview with my co-author to flesh out the final chapters of the book you're presently reading. I proceeded to attack my daily to-do list, tackling the most important item first.

So many times, we get sidetracked when something doesn't go right. In disgust, we throw away the entire day. Screw that. You control the narrative; you control the day. Get back to work living your ideal life. Your family deserves it. Your clients deserve it. And, most importantly, you deserve it.

THE MAKEOVER METHOD™

You control the narrative; you control the day.

MADEOVER

Katie really enjoys yoga and had been trying to get me to attend class with her for quite some time. She kept talking about how she thought it would be a great workout for me. Now, as a guy who used to play college ball and whose workouts were weight training focused, yoga did not seem like it would be a workout at all. But I finally caved and joined her for a class; it made her happy, and I figured I would just tell her it wasn't my thing, but at least I could say I tried.

I could not have been more wrong about how "easy" I initially thought yoga would be. The room was heated to ninety degrees, and I was sweating buckets, which I would have been doing even if the yoga practice wasn't hard, but it definitely was. Long story short, that first class kicked my ass, and I was sore for days after. But I really enjoyed the heat, the sweating, the hour of mental focus and the five minutes of rest and reflection at the end of each session. I now consider it essential to work a yoga class into my schedule at least three times a week. It's as important for my mind as it is for my body. The lesson: don't be afraid to try new things!

Your brand engine can be described as your daily habits and routines that, over time, lead you to the results you desire. It's where you amplify the power of a stronger mindset combined with the proven business-related principles of building a powerful business image. The first layer of The Makeover Method™ (mindset) will determine what your potential ceiling is, what your potential capabilities are. How well you solve that first layer will determine whether or not you ultimately reach a business that creates $100,000 per year or $100,000 per month. The final product is a result of your mindset plus your relationships plus your capabilities plus your skills. How skilled you are is a huge component, but mastering your daily habits, your engine, is the catalyst—the amplifier—that takes everything to the next level. If you do all the work to increase your confidence, negate your limiting beliefs, and prove your business model but your daily habits and routines suck, you won't be able to reach your full potential.

Part of my daily habits involves going with the flow. That's why, on the morning I slept through my alarm, I didn't maintain the attitude that the day was ruined when I might have done just that a year ago. I stopped attaching emotion to the way things went. If a media interview bombed, I'd take some sort of lesson from it. If I got a flat tire, I wondered who I might meet at the tire shop. It became about turning inconvenience into opportunity.

When I arrived in Hollywood for an interview on *Good Morning La La Land* a few months ago, I realized I'd forgotten the power cord for my laptop. The old me would have seen the need to head out and buy a new one as a huge inconvenience. Instead, I chose to see my Uber ride, stuck in traffic for an hour and a half, as an opportunity to talk with Nathan Ortega, my podcast guy. We worked through our next few opportunities together and used that time effectively. Instead of bitching about my drive to the Apple store in Santa Monica, I used it to my advantage and got something done.

When Katie and I met at the Hillsboro Air Show in 2001, neither of us had ever attended before. We were both essentially there to drink beer and hang out. What are the odds? Twenty-four hours prior, neither of us was planning to be there. Eighteen years later, we're married with two kids. You simply never know where something is going to lead.

This is why the engine is crucial to your business and life. It's how you get some amazing things done. And, the really big things don't happen overnight; they take time. As Tony Robbins says, people dramatically overestimate what's possible to get done in a year and underestimate what's possible to get done in ten.

In *Deep Work*, Cal Newport told the story of a guy whose job was to translate complex ancient texts. His goal was to translate one page per day. His routine was to dedicate a focused ninety minutes in the morning and then take a ninety-minute break. Most days, he'd work for ninety minutes, take a ninety-minute break, and then work for another focused ninety minutes. That's it. Occasionally he'd get another round in, and sometimes he didn't, but that was his day. Someone asked him how he got through all the texts, and he replied with the details of his routine, which he was consistent with for over ten years. In many ways, it comes back to Tim Ferriss's 4-hour workweek concept. His DEAL approach is: Define what you want, Eliminate everything that doesn't need to be in your routine, Automate as much as you can, and Liberate yourself from the traditional 9-5 life.

When you look at the challenges many are experiencing, you realize how common they are: anxiety, depression, a sense of overwhelm, and burnout. The fact is, most of those problems lessen or go away altogether once you have clarity, confidence, and are taking action. You have days when you feel like you're making real headway, and those are the days that tend to "cure" a temporary state of overwhelm, indecision, or anxiety.

When entrepreneurs don't feel like they're making progress toward their goals, they feel depressed. When they're making progress toward their mission, they have the opposite feeling. They have the sense that everything's working. Sometimes, taking a "sick day" is what's truly necessary to solve the lack-of-clarity challenge. As action takers, we tend to completely overwhelm ourselves and, in many ways, that overwhelm is, therefore, a self-created problem. It helps tremendously just to push Pause. It doesn't even have to be a full sick day. Sometimes a half day is all that's needed. But you need some carved-out time to focus on what you're doing, the biggest priority, and the one thing you can get clear on. Then, focus your time and attention on that one thing. There are weeks when I have 200 tasks on my to-do list. We all have thoughts and internal conversations, and those conversations can become really noisy if left unaddressed. We all crave confidence. This was one of the first big lessons I learned in the Strategic Coach program. Confidence is a byproduct of having the courage to take the first step. In order to take that first step, we have to have clarity on what it is.

So, how do I run The Makeover Engine™ for myself and what does this mean to you?

If you think about it, a car's engine doesn't make the car move, decide which direction to go, or determine how fast or slow you are going. The engine itself needs to be maintained properly to run, but making the car move, deciding whether to turn left or right, and whether to go fast or slow is up to the driver.

Your brand engine is the same. You are the driver, and you are in control. Your engine is made up of a set of parts that can be throttled faster or slower at any time, and you can even determine if parts need to be replaced or enhanced.

THE MAKEOVER ENGINE™

Remember that my engine is mine, and your engine is yours. As such, you get to determine what your engine looks like. But I'll share mine with you as an example. I've included below the hand-drawn sketch of my original engine, and it remains similar today. This is the engine of my life, the actions I take consistently to get everything I want in business and in life. It's changed everything for me, and I hope that your engine will do the same for you. I used to feel anxious all the time, like I was never getting enough done. Until I said, "Enough! This is crazy, let me control each day and see where it leads me."

It's led me to my ideal lifestyle.

Let me be clear, there is an internal system and checklist for all of this. It's the only way I can be consistent with any of it.

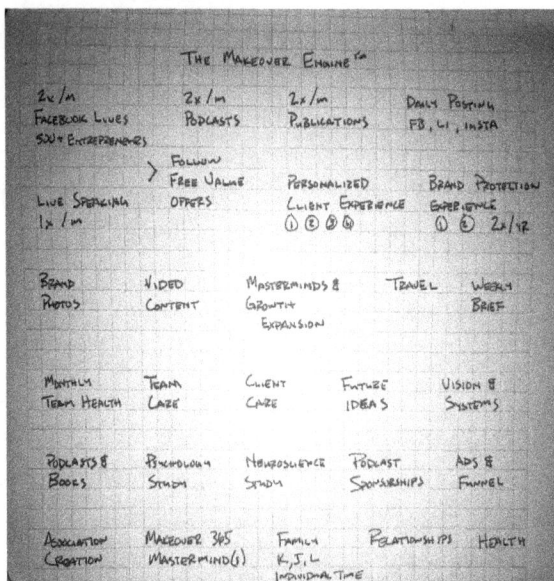

Here are the parts of my engine from the bottom up:

- Healthy
- Relationships
- Family Time—Together and Individually
- Makeover 365 Masterminds
- Association Creation
- Ads and Funnel
- Podcast Sponsorships
- Neuroscience Study
- Psychology Study
- Podcasts and Books
- Weekly Brief
- Travel
- Masterminds and Growth Expansion
- Video Content
- Brand Photos

- Brand Protection Experience (2x per year)
- Personalized Client Experience (4x/12-stage process)
- Free Value, Courses, Offerings
- Daily Social Posting
- Publications (2x per month)
- Podcasts (2x per month)
- Live Speaking (1x per month)
- Facebook Lives—500+ Entrepreneurs, 2x per month

The creation of your engine can feel very overwhelming at first, which is why you need to think it all through, and assign a system and checklist to each part of your engine that's scheduled.

IT CAN ALL GET DONE…CONSISTENTLY.

I know because I do it.

My engine is the result of the evolution of years of work, years of floundering around, years of not getting the business and life I wanted. When I put this all together and ran it consistently, everything changed. The brand engine transformed my business and saved my life, quite literally.

With this engine in place, I have tens of thousands of people finding out that I exist on a weekly basis. People are not confused about what I do and how they can begin a relationship with me. Over time, my ideal clients emerge and ask questions. They chase me instead of me having to chase them.

It was a lot of work to put all of this together, and I remember feeling like I was running out of time. I needed income *immediately*! But the truth is, it's the best thing I've ever done for my business and life.

THE MAKEOVER METHOD™

Document everything, and attach a system you can consistently implement to everything you do.

MADEOVER

Document everything, and attach a system you can consistently implement to everything you do. Focus on what you want, eliminate everything that doesn't get you closer to the life you want, and then run the engine every single day. That's the secret so many of you are looking for. It's not magic, it's clarity and consistency.

Part of mastering your daily habits is determining which habit you're mastering at any one point in time. For people with no daily habits in place (or inconsistent ones at best), trying to incorporate six or seven new ones all at once is often a recipe for failure in every area. So start with one. When you're comfortable with that one as a daily habit, add another.

As part of my daily habit of journaling, I list out on the left-hand side of the page all the to-dos that need to happen in order to get to my ideal lifestyle. Making this list helps me determine what tasks on that list have to be completed by me, and which I can delegate. Unexpectedly, I found that this activity requires an intentional questioning of my own belief system in many areas: does this particular task actually have to be done by me, does it have to be done at all, or is either belief just a story I'm telling myself?

This list includes tasks such as meditation and journaling, working out, eating a healthy diet, family time, individual time with Katie, and time with each of my kids. I can't delegate any of those tasks. Live speaking, mindset work, client communication, and Facebook Lives are also critical for me, and they can't be delegated. Posting three or four times a day on Facebook doesn't have to happen, even though I once told myself a story that it does. Social media posts don't necessarily have to be written by me long-term, but they do have to be based on my philosophy. So, if I'm going to delegate that task, it has to be done by someone who really knows me and what I stand for.

This engine is not about being perfect, and sometimes you need to break the routine. Several months ago, I went on a road trip. I had four or five clients with whom I could definitely have been communicating better. I also had four or five clients whose new brands were rolling out, and those rollouts weren't going as smoothly as I would have liked. My clients were fine with what was going on, but I knew it could be a million times smoother and faster. I didn't have anxiety, per se, but I felt minor frustration over all the things that needed be done. Katie was at the beach and came home with the flu, so I was solely responsible for the kids' needs for two days straight starting the minute I got home. Instead of coming to my office the first day, I took the morning off and said, "I'm just going to run some errands, fill up the gas tank, and get the car washed." I was wondering about the fact that I felt okay "breaking the rules" of my daily structure even though I had so much to do.

In 2008, I used to break the traditional rules just to see what would happen. For example, what would happen if I had 500 emails and I just highlighted and deleted all of them? I remember wondering, as a kid, what would happen if, while riding my bike down a steep hill, I wiggled the handlebars really fast. The result: I flipped over and totally wrecked my face by skidding on it. So that didn't work out well. But I was always willing to try shit just to see what would happen. There have been a few times I'm lucky I wasn't killed, to be honest. I hated fruits and vegetables growing up, and when I was in college one of my buddies dared me to try a green pepper on pizza. I surprisingly thought, "This tastes pretty good!" and that made me wonder what other fruits and vegetables might taste good. So I started eating strawberries.

On this morning, when my instinct was to force myself to head straight to the office even though my mind was foggy and I wasn't focused, I decided to do something different. I took an hour or two and took care of some tasks that felt more in alignment. And you know what? Everything worked out just fine! By the time I got to the office, I was refocused and got more done in three hours than I likely would have in six, had I forced myself to go straight in.

Belief in what you're doing and a commitment to determine the most effective strategy *right now* for your product or service is paramount. Don't worry about what might be a great strategy in six months or a year. Consider where your ideal customers are right now, and how you can best serve them.

There are brands that only use chatbots, and they make $1 million per year. For example, ManyChat uses a Facebook chatbot to drive all their traffic and handle all their marketing calls. There are also brands that do everything through email, using a bunch of tools and widgets (of which there are about 10,000 to choose from). There's an online candy store that allows customers to put together their own customized candy bags. Which approach and platform is right for you? What's the perfect mix that's going to help you reach your ideal clients, provide value through your unique package, and get you to your ideal lifestyle?

You do your thing, and the type of person you're trying to attract will be attracted to you. Your primary job, therefore, isn't to be out there posting like crazy trying to find needles in a huge haystack. Your primary job is to have massive clarity on exactly who you're trying to attract. Focus your engine so you are speaking directly to that one person.

As I continue to hone my daily habits, I've put in place a few new team members to help take tasks off my plate that do not need to be completed by me. I'm also very protective of my time and mental energy. I know that through building systems, cultivating my team, and mastering my daily habits, this is the most disciplined I've been in a long time. Honestly, it's not easy. It's dead simple, but it's not easy. These changes, however, will allow me to have greater focus and impact for my clients while my business grows to new heights, and knowing that keeps me pushing forward through the resistance each and every day.

Now it's your time to create your new reality.

You can find all of The Makeover Method™ resources on our website:

https://themakeovermaster.com/resources

YOUR NEW REALITY

*Time is an illusion created by our mind, five
minutes ago and the end of the Roman
Empire are equally over. Focus on the
present, it's all you can control.*

Reality can change in an instant. I remember
watching my son almost get run over by a car once.
While it wasn't as close of a call as it might sound, a
car was coming out of an alley, and he was standing in its
path. He was probably only four at the time. We were in
Seattle, and we had just gone to a park or a museum. I
yelled, "Hey, Jeff! Slow down!" because there was an alley
right there, and just then a car came screaming out of the
alley. It missed him by six feet or so, but the moment still
had a huge impact. The message was: we have one life.

When we first moved into our current house, Jeff was
five. There is a cemetery next to our house, and every time
we drove by it, he asked, "What's that place with all the
rocks?" He would not let go of this question; he's
relentless. I have no idea where he gets that. He became
obsessed with going to the "place with all the rocks."
Finally, Katie said, "Well, I guess I have to take him to the

cemetery!" She took him and talked to him about people's headstones. Some were flat and flush to the ground, and some were taller. Afterward, Jeff said, "Thanks, Mom. I feel better now that I know what's going on here."

One evening shortly afterward, we were putting him to bed, and he said, "When I die, I just really want to have a big rock." I think that's what it comes down to for most people. In Jeff's mind, the size of the headstone represented how successful the person was. I think about that often—how big is your potential? I just want to have a really big rock at the end of all of this. I don't care how big my actual headstone is. I just want someone to be able to say, "That guy actually made a difference—not only to himself and his family but to me."

Regardless of the age at which I predicted I'd die during our first Strategic Coach meeting, whenever I do leave this Earth, I will miss obvious things like Katie and my kids. And, while it might sound a bit kooky, I'll actually miss the struggle and the striving. I'll miss the things that made or still make me uncomfortable but helped me grow so much as a person. I'll miss goal-setting. I'll miss saying, "Here's what I want to accomplish, and I don't know how the fuck I'm going to get there, but I'm just going to take action until it happens." I'll miss giving back to other people. Part of the reason I'm writing this book is that, without it, there's no legacy.

At some point, I got my head straight. I realized that I had written the chapters of my life up to this point. I remember thinking, "How do I want my story to end? What will my remaining chapter of life say about me?"

Sanja, my lead designer, sent me a great YouTube video the other day. It showcased the hardest video game ever, featuring a guy—almost like a Super Mario character—who just kept getting killed, but kept getting back up. The game was impossibly hard.

Sanja's simple introduction to the video: "This is you."

Over the past decade, I became obsessed with figuring out how to realize my ideal lifestyle. I never stopped thinking about it. I'd see things in day-to-day life and think about how they related to something I was working on. The constant driving force for me has been that I have two kids who I want to have a role model who shows them what it takes to go after their vision—and that it's absolutely possible to reach it. My commitment has never wavered (at least not for more than a few days or weeks). No matter the obstacle, I've found a way over, around, or through it.

Five years ago, I wanted to surpass my expectations for myself. My mindset today realizes that striving for that only represents comparison, and it's far too related to caring about what other people think to work for me anymore. Today, just as in the game of golf, it's about meeting the potential that comes from playing against the course. I wake up every day, and I give it my best shot. Some days go as planned, and some don't. From the very beginning, I had a vision of my idea lifestyle. I knew it included working where, when, and with whom I wanted. No stress. Unlimited financial resources. Spontaneous trips with my family. I had no idea it would be such a grind to get there. And frankly, had I known, I likely wouldn't have started because I wasn't the same man then that I am today. If someone could have said, "It will take nearly ten years and feel like hell, but at the end, you'll have the lifestyle you desire and complete peace and an impact on the world," I would have pushed forward. But no one can ever predict that with any level of true certainty.

I didn't hit the lottery. I earned it. I took the time to commit to the life of freedom that I wanted.

Make peace with the fact that you don't know everything. You never will. You're going to learn something today, tomorrow, and again next week. Looking back, I wouldn't change any of it because the process of going through it all led me to where I am today. I'm a better person. I'm more knowledgeable. I've made mistakes through which I've learned so many great lessons. Losing money and doing things the "wrong" way shaped me. Even if I could rewind and pay someone $30,000 to teach it all to me from the beginning, while I might have made money faster, and I might have solved some of my self-confidence issues earlier, I'd still have a completely different story. Maybe I wouldn't have had quite the struggle, but I'm at a place where I'm truly grateful for it. All of it. My gratefulness boils down to being able to relate to other entrepreneurs.

When somebody tells me they're struggling to make their business work, I really and truly get it.

I'm in alignment with my truest self. I'm excited about what I'm doing. I don't remember what podcast I was listening to, I think it was Oprah Winfrey's Masterclass, but there was a comment that if something happened once, it could happen again. In that moment, I realized that I've made $40,000 in a day before. And there was no reason I couldn't consistently do that again. Being in alignment and excited about what I'm doing creates a massive energy ball that makes me not want to stop some days. I can't sleep some nights. I just want to keep going. But I also have the recognition that sometimes I need to stop because it's never going to end. I used to not want my days to end out of fear. Now I don't want them to end out of excitement.

Sure, I've also had those moments, even in the past year, when I went weeks or months without a sale. Interestingly, I had a sense of calm about it, and I believe that came from the self-confidence of knowing that I can make it through anything if I made it through two periods of going completely broke. That newfound alignment automatically appears once you've taken the time to consciously put every piece of The Makeover Method™ in place.

I'm grateful to have gone through what ultimately formed the basis for The Makeover Method™. I followed society's rules for a long time. It's no longer about the money. To be clear, I will want the money because the money represents tremendous freedom and a greater impact I can have on the lives of my clients, my family, my friends, and my community. You can do a lot of things and make a lot of moves when you're earning $300,000 per month. But I can honestly say that I wouldn't rush out and buy a house or a new watch the way I would have ten years ago.

Back then, I would have gone all Nicolas Cage— lifestyle inflation whereby you make the money and keep inflating your lifestyle. But when things turn and the money stops, you go broke. I thought you were supposed to inflate your lifestyle in accordance with or parallel to your income. Why did I think that was necessary? Perhaps I thought that when you get money, you buy a big house and cars. I thought that there was nowhere to go but up. That was before I got punched in the face. It's like Mike Tyson said: "Everybody's got a plan until you get punched in the face." I've had that punched-in-the-face experience a couple of times now, and I don't need to repeat it.

Back in the day when I had $160,000 in my checking account at any point in time, we'd go out for $200 dinners five nights a week. We wouldn't do that today. We'd go to nice dinners, but back then I was spending money just to spend money. Perhaps I was trying to convince myself that I'd made it. When Katie and I went to Mexico once back in the day, I think I spent $8,500 in four days, which is actually quite hard (and yet easy) to do. You kind of have to be trying to piss away money. Today, if I wanted to take a nice vacation, I would. But I wouldn't up the price on everything. I don't even know who the hell I was trying to impress!

I'd rather be financially broke than spiritually broke any day. To be sure, I've been both. Being spiritually broke is a miserable feeling, and it's way worse than being financially broke. Money just teaches you something about yourself. It teaches you how to be resourceful. It also teaches you that, in the end, money isn't the answer you're seeking.

People ask what the secret is to my "luck." The secret is this: decide exactly who you are and what you want, and take consistent action every single day until you get there. Do that, and I promise that you'll find yourself exactly as lucky as I am.

You can find all of The Makeover Method™ resources on our website:

https://themakeovermaster.com/resources

ACKNOWLEDGEMENTS

This book is the culmination of a decade-plus-long journey to build my ideal lifestyle. It would not exist without the love and support of my wife, family, friends, mentors, coaches, and team.

Katie Bunn Young, I am forever grateful to you and your unwavering belief in me through even our darkest days and nights.

Mitch Miller and Macaully Ryan, the founders of Opposed Media Co., the rabbit hole ran deeper than I ever imaged, and I am eternally grateful for your gift of mentorship and guidance. It has changed my business and life forever.

Clay Moffat, The B.A.D Entrepreneur, your wizardry mindset conditioning literally saved my life. Working with you has set me (and my family) free from the burnout, anxiety, and depression I suffered from when we met. You have shown me the path to live the life of my dreams with continual expansion.

Sanja Stojkovic, you stuck with me and believed in me before I believed in myself. I will forever have your back for all you have accomplished (and been through) with me. None of this would exist without your knowledge and mad skills. I can only imagine what is yet to come for our families and us together.

Wayne and Joanne Young, you have shown me what it looks like to support and love a child unconditionally. I would not be the man I am today without you.

I want to thank my close inner-circle of local friends, even though I "disappeared" for a couple of years to make my business and life work together. Dan, Jeff, Seth, Brian, and Ryan, you guys and your families are the truest of friends.

There are so many other relationships, including both in-person and virtual friends and mentors in my entrepreneurial inner circle I want to thank. Each one of you has played a role, shared insights, or helped guide me in some way. I am sure right after this book is printed, I will realize who I forgot to put on this list.

Michael Tietje, Dorothy Illson, Paul Halme, Zachary Babcock, Tim Nussbeck, Mike Kemski, Jan Jagen, Desislava Dobreva, Andrew Mercier, Ulyses Osuna, Fanny Myth, Bobby Stocks, Ariane de Melo, Karla Stefan Singson, Amir Pozderac, Todd Ballenger, Tom Griffith, Dan Sullivan, Gary Vaynerchuk, Tim Ferris, Russell Brunson.

Elizabeth Lyons, I have no words. Truly, this book would not have gotten done without the help of "The Entrepreneurs' Author." Your ability to draw out my story and co-author this book was invaluable to me. This experience with you has been profound in my life, and this story will find and help someone discover their ideal lifestyle and make it through their own struggles because of you. I'm forever grateful to have worked with you on this book, and for our friendship.

You have all had a tremendous influence on my business, life, and journey. Thank you.